BOMBS, BULLETS, AND THE TANK AT THE OFFICE

ISBN: 979-8-5824305-1-3

Library of Congress Control Number: TXu 2-219-431

Book design by The Book Designers, bookdesigners.com

Printed by Kindle Direct Publishing in the United States of America.

First printing edition 2020.

BOMBS, BULLETS, AND THE TANK AT THE OFFICE

Protecting America on Diplomacy's Front Lines

Carol Stricker

DEDICATION

This book is dedicated to you, dear reader, for opening up this book. I hope that you will also open your hearts and minds to the idea that ideals — and patience and persistence in their pursuit — can make a difference in this world. At its best, America stands for truth, justice, accountability, and equal treatment and opportunity for all. At their best, Americans are known for their compassion, and the sacrifices they've made for a better world — think of two world wars Americans fought and died in, and of the Marshall Plan that rebuilt Europe and gave it peace after the war's devastation. I hope that you will come to value the diplomacy that embodies these ideals, and honor the sacrifices and service of the women and men who practice it by supporting them and their work.

This book was difficult for me to write. I had flashbacks to difficult, scary times as I revisited my decades of diplomatic service. I have witnessed the positive power of American diplomacy and democracy during those years, though, and feel compelled to tell my story.

Today I am dismayed to see diplomacy and democracy under attack, but I refuse to give up on America. I think back to a colleague at the U.S. Embassy in Tbilisi, Georgia in

2005. This former *citizen of the Soviet Union* volunteered to serve in harm's way at the U.S. Embassy in Baghdad to help staff our growing mission. His father was a respected village school master in Georgia in the early 1900s, an educated man who could and would think for himself. When the Soviets invaded Georgia in 1921, they immediately "disappeared" him as a threat to their regime. My colleague, despite being subjected to years of anti-American propaganda during the Cold War, told me, "Your country freed my country, and brought truth and democracy to it. I want to go to Baghdad and help America."

This loyalty to American ideals can neither be bought nor bombed into existence. It is a testament to what America once stood for in the world — and can stand for again. It is the America that I was proud to represent as a diplomat. It is the America of united, informed citizens that the United States and the world need today — the informed person who thinks for himself or herself, acts for the common good, and does not blindly follow party propaganda or cult of personality. Freedom is not free, and democracy must be continuously nurtured or it will be lost.

This book is also dedicated to my family, friends and colleagues who supported me and these ideals throughout my career — and to all who continue to support them in these trying times. This book is dedicated to every member of the U.S. Foreign Service, past, present and future, in gratitude for their hard work and sacrifices for America and Americans.

Finally, this book is dedicated to Michelle Deney O'Connor, Bill Bultemeier and others in the U.S. Foreign Service who gave their lives for these ideals[P1]. With no weapons other than the power of words and ideals they went into harm's way, and paid the ultimate price to help defend and protect America and the American way of life.

"Greater love hath no man than this, that a man lay down his life for his country"

CONTENTS

1

THE WHY OF THE BOOK

I joined the U.S. Department of State, *the United States' premier foreign affairs agency,* in 1984 to help make the world a better place. I believe in the American ideals of working to "form a more perfect Union" of good governance, justice, peace and prosperity. I believe in the ideals that the Founding Fathers of these United States fought and died for, that "all . . . are created equal" and that we have the inalienable rights of life, liberty and the pursuit of happiness. Finally, I support diplomacy and the Department of State's goals to share and advance these American ideals to create a more secure, democratic and prosperous world for the benefit of the American people and the global community.

American diplomats are also known as "*Foreign Service Officers.*" I was willing, in *foreign* countries far from home, to *serve* as a *professional,* to engage with the world to protect the United States, its people and its national interests, and to make the world a better place.

To be clear, good governance means abiding by the rule of law, pursuing equal justice for all, and insisting upon truth, transparency and accountability from the government to the governed. Good governance includes the freedoms of speech, press, assembly and religion. Peace and prosperity are prerequisites for, and a result of, good governance, and both require constant care and attention.

American diplomats, supporting the interests of the U.S. government, work to attain these goals for all, and not just for a few countries or for a country's elites. Diplomats also support good health (eradicating malaria, fighting against Ebola, Severe Acute Respiratory Syndrome or SARS and now Covid 19). They promote education and the equal opportunity for all that can lead to prosperity and thus a safer world. They fight for security: for the security of the individual so he or she need not worry about being harassed, harmed or even killed due to race, religion, ethnicity or ideals. They fight for security against terrorism, the scourge of our time. The fodder for terrorists is youth with no hope or opportunity. Diplomats bring hope and opportunity to the world. As I recount my diplomatic journey, I hope that you will share my pride in what U.S. diplomacy has accomplished to make the world a safer and better place. The world is not perfect, but I, with my diplomatic colleagues, have helped many countries move towards peace, prosperity and good governance.

After 20 years as a American diplomat, most spent overseas, I am now back home in the United States and am dismayed to see American ideals trampled upon: basic democratic institutions such as the Congress and the Judiciary maligned and undermined, and people who serve being denigrated and harassed. These are dark times. President Trump is on record as equating dissent with disloyalty and ignoring truths if they are inconvenient to his world view. He praises dictators, vilifies our allies, and attacks war heroes, diplomats, the free press, the independent judiciary, and anyone else who does not agree with him and his agenda. I am disheartened by members of Congress who constitute an independent branch of government and are sworn to uphold the Constitution, but instead rubber stamp every presidential motion. They practice political grandstanding and squabble while ignoring urgent issues of the day, from endless wars to climate change to racism, poverty and hunger — including among children — in this first-world country. And I am appalled that peaceful protestors can be tear gassed and fired upon as they exercise their Constitutional rights — in the nation's capital — to tackle the injustice of racism that still has such a pervasive and negative influence in the United States today. Finally, I find it a national disgrace that almost half of U.S. citizens — *in this government of the people, by the people and for the people* — don't vote in presidential elections. At the same time, U.S. diplomats advocate for and support free and fair elections as crucial to helping strengthen democracies and promote good governance across the globe.

And let us not forget the "fourth estate," the mainstream press and social media that are today's influencers. At their best they are advocates for truth, openness and accountability and can be a window on a wider world. At their worst they offer us opinion as fact, spread untruths and incite hatred and bigotry that divide and weaken us.

This book, then, is in defense of American ideals, and the diplomats who seek to nurture these ideals and share them with the world. My final Chapter is a call to action, outlining the tools I supported as a diplomat to achieve positive change in countries across the globe. Dear reader, please join me in using these to effect positive change in these United States right now.

This book touches upon history but raises critical current

issues by way of truths gained from my experiences in over two dozen countries across the globe over my career. The chapters track my career through my tours abroad and at the State Department's headquarters in Washington D.C. To jump start what I hope will prove to be a thoughtful exercise, I begin, in Chapter Two, with a short "true/false quiz." I offer truths, falsehoods and the urban myths about diplomacy that have acquired a life of their own. This will test your knowledge of diplomacy and provide food for thought as you join me on my diplomatic journey. For a glimpse of the history that grounds this book and my ideals, I offer you the following quotes:

> Freedom is never more than one generation away from extinction. We didn't pass it to our children in the bloodstream. It must be fought for, protected, and handed on for them to do the same. [Ronald Reagan]

> True patriotism springs from a belief in the dignity of the individual, freedom and equality not only for Americans but for all people on earth, universal brotherhood and good will, and a constant and earnest striving toward the principles and ideals on which this country was founded. [Eleanor Roosevelt]

> Ask not what your country can do for you, ask what you can do for your country. [John F. Kennedy]

In Chapters Three and Four I talk of my first two assignments in Bamako, Mali and Montreal, Canada. In these two very different countries, I learned both my job and a seminal truth that, despite differences in looks, preferences and policies, at heart, people are all alike. The African fathers, the mothers raising their children under Soviet oppression, all just wanted a better life and the hope of a better future for their children.

In Chapters Five and Six I discuss life and work in Ukraine. Helping establish a new embassy in Ukraine shortly after the fall of the Soviet Union in 1991 gave me some thought-provoking insights, leavened with humor, that kept me and my fellow diplomats going through trying times. I talk about almost 2000 nuclear warheads and weapons eliminated in the country and Ukraine's progress towards democracy and rule of law that made all of our hard work and sacrifices worthwhile. I also touch upon the opportunities squandered at this time of great upheaval and change. This diplomatic assignment highlighted a truth that I witnessed time and time again: *if you want your government to succeed, you must prioritize and clearly delineate its goals and then make sure it has the staff, funding and other resources to achieve them.*

WE TOO OFTEN COMPLAIN THAT OUR GOVERNMENT DOES NOT SERVE US WELL – BUT DO WE SERVE AND SUPPORT IT?

In Chapter Seven, I focus on two tours in Washington, D.C. The first was as a Special Assistant to the Assistant Secretary of State for the Bureau of Oceans and International Environmental and Scientific Affairs (OES) Bureau. The second was as an analyst in the Office of Sanctions Policy for the Bureau of Economic, Business, and Agricultural Affairs (EB). Both tours exemplified the best of government practitioners and practices. I advocated for and advanced American interests, ensuring that the concerns of all — from businesses of all sizes, to advocacy groups and non-profits, from highly paid lobbyists to the general public — were heard and considered. No one got everything he or she wanted, but everyone had their say. I worked with responsible, accountable officers acting with integrity and honor, who came to the best decisions possible in working to implement U.S. Government policies and programs. Their efforts helped protect the health of the planet, stop the spread of terrorism, foster democracy and the rule to law and otherwise work towards a better world. They openly and honestly explained their work to the U.S. Congress, various interest groups and the general public.

Returning to Africa in Chapter Eight, I provide some background to this complex continent. In Chapters Nine and Ten, I discuss my Africa Bureau "Rover" tour, during which I filled shocking staffing gaps in ten countries across Africa over two years. This tour graphically highlights the costs of doing diplomacy — or anything else — with insufficient personnel and resources. The next time you wait for hours at a government office, please remember that there are good people there, but that they may well be woefully understaffed. To bring this concept closer to home, think of your own office or workplace. How effective would you be if you were missing a third to one-half of your staff, but your workload kept growing?

Chapter Eleven covers my 2000-2002 assignment to Niamey, Niger. I address the issue of terrorism, which tragically hit the United States on 9/11/2001. Life as we knew it, and diplomacy as I'd practiced it, were forever changed.

In Chapter Twelve, I move on to the U.S. Consulate in Frankfurt, Germany. At the time, this mission was the U.S. government's fifth largest in the world, and a powerhouse of U.S. interagency and multinational coordination. As the Consulate's Deputy Director of the Regional Support Center (RSC), I supported and strengthened our under-funded and understaffed embassies in the former Soviet Union, as well as throughout Europe and in Africa. I provided training and focused guidance, and also supplied many U.S. diplomatic missions with U.S. military furnishings and equipment that were surplus to U.S. military needs after the end of the Cold War.

I also served in Frankfurt as the Acting Management Officer for half a year providing support to over two dozen separate agencies and organizations and almost 800 personnel. These people capably supported U.S. government strategic national interests — everything from countering terrorism and international crimes like narco- and human trafficking, to providing consular services to American citizens, and particularly to the large U.S. military population in Germany. The inter-agency, and even international coordination that U.S. agencies exhibited daily was a perfect example of how the United States is much stronger and more effective in reaching common goals when it is united with allies.

In Chapter Thirteen I return to the former Soviet Union, to the now independent Republic of Georgia. I provide insights into this proud nation 15 years after the fall of the Soviet Union and Georgia's declaration of independence. I also talk about the continuing challenges Georgia faced, including ongoing Russian interference in the country.

Chapter Fourteen covers my last tour of duty, back in the United States. I served as Associate Dean for the School of Languages Studies at the State Department's premier training institution, the Foreign Service Institute (FSI). FSI is also the State Department's think tank addressing key questions: what do U.S. diplomats need to know, what do they need to do, and what are the tools (tech, training, etc.) required to help them meet these needs as efficiently and effectively as possible. In short, how can we best support our diplomats so they can best serve the United States and make the world a better place for the peace, prosperity and security of the United Sates and the world.

So I present to you the idea, based on my decades of experience and truths witnessed on-the-ground, that the basics of American democracy, including rule of law, honor, integrity, truth, transparency and accountability of the government to the governed, matter. That our democratic institutions and the people who serve them deserve our support, protection and appreciation. That freedom is not free, but must be daily nurtured and supported so it does not founder here at home, and so it can foster a more perfect world. Democracy is not guaranteed and our democratic institutions, including free and fair elections, an independent judiciary and a free and independent press, must be protected by an engaged, informed, and active electorate.

In America, despite our rich democratic traditions and rule of law, educated population, wealth of natural resources, good neighbors and so many other assets, I worry that we risk losing the democracy and good governance that we have worked towards for over 200 years. Uncivil discourse, government misinformation, lack of accountability and transparency, attacks on government institutions and the people serving in them, hate-mongering and worse, are undermining the very foundations of our democracy. In my final chapter Fourteen, I offer a challenge, and a call to action:

Support diplomacy and the diplomats *who are a part of the U.S. national security apparatus that best serve the United States in their work towards peace, prosperity and security for the United States and the world.* Support their hard work, creativity, and passion to make the world a better place, for the United States, its citizens and for the greater world. And most importantly, support democracy and good governance here at home. Fight against the hypocrisy that calls for democracy and good governance in other countries while we let both be attacked and undermined on the home front. Citizens were the power behind getting women the vote, the civil rights movement and other successes of democratic rule, and united we can still make a difference. When you see something wrong, speak up and speak out. Together we continue on our path towards a more perfect union.

2

TRUE, FALSE, OR URBAN MYTH

I offer this chapter as a small test of your knowledge of diplomacy, and to address many of the misconceptions that persist about diplomacy and its practitioners. I hope this will serve as food for thought and that you will take to heart some of this information and these ideas. There will be no test at the end of this book, but I hope to convince you — and will challenge you — to support democracy, diplomacy and the people who support and defend both.

Simply put, diplomats work to create a more secure, democratic, and prosperous world for the benefit of the United States, its citizens and the international community. They do this by listening and looking; analyzing and making informed, reasoned decisions; working collegially with all concerned parties; and then taking action. Diplomats are professionals who use their knowledge, skills and abilities — and patience and persistence — to support the good, alleviate or eliminate the bad and above all, try to make the good self-sustaining. Diplomats must understand the world, and particularly, the country to which they are assigned.

They must bring all their talents and creativity to identifying and addressing problems, and speak truth to power to ensure that America's strategic national interests are not ignored. Their painstaking hard work may not always pay off immediately in a difficult and dangerous world, yet it is nonetheless work that must be done. So I present you with this overview of some of the truths — and myths — about diplomats and diplomacy. This section is highly endnoted, but do not let that daunt you. As promised, there will be no test on this material. Rather, I provide these endnotes for you, dear reader, in case you'd like to delve deeper into any of these interesting issues.

T/F: Diplomats are "striped-pants cookie pushers." Well, I've never owned a pair of striped pants. I have, however, done my share of receptions (cookies rarely involved), where I've gained valuable insights into and information on current events, people and issues — and tried to influence same.

I was at a reception hosted by the U.S. Embassy in Burundi in support of international efforts (1997-98) to stop the genocide there. Think Philip Gourevitch's book *We Wish to Inform You that Tomorrow We Will Be Killed* or the film *Hotel Rwanda*. Burundi is Rwanda's less famous next-door neighbor, with the same problems. I was literally struck speechless when an official came up to me and said, "If we just killed all of ***them*** as we did ten years ago, we wouldn't have this problem today." The murder of even one person on the basis of race, religion, ethnicity, gender, orientation — or any other reason at all — is unconscionable. While we didn't stop the genocide overnight, I was honored to be part of the process that stopped the killings in the end.

T/F: "Diplomats are cookie pushers." On this, I'll let you decide. In the early morning hours of December 23, 2000, in Niamey, Niger, the head of the embassy's Defense Attaché Office — my colleague and good friend Bill Bultemeier — was killed in the carjacking of his clearly marked diplomatic vehicle.[1] The embassy's Marine Security Guard Detachment Commander Christopher McNeely was seriously injured as well as he dove to cover Bill and help him. On Christmas Eve, Bill's family, happily waiting for him to come home . . . instead got the grim news of his death.

As this tragedy was unfolding, I hoped to provide some small cheer to Christopher's children as they learned of their father's injuries, so I sent the Marines to my house to get my Christmas care package for them. They and the Marines got the wonderful Christmas cookies my Mom and younger sister had made, along with hot chocolate and other treats not available in Niamey. The Marines also managed to put the McNeelys' Christmas presents onto the plane that took Chris and his family (and transferred Bill's body) to the U.S. military hospital at Landstuhl, Germany. The Landstuhl staff collected presents for the McNeely children too, but the children's best present that Christmas was their father's successful recovery after surgery.

The U.S. military hospital in Landstuhl, Germany featured in a second "cookie pushing" incident. During my service at the U.S. Consulate in Frankfurt, Germany, mission personnel gladly baked cookies for our troops injured in Afghanistan and Iraq who were receiving treatment at this hospital a short drive from the U.S. Consulate. We were shocked, though, when we began to receive requests for underwear and socks for the wounded warriors there. If a person could give up an arm, leg or more for his or her country, the least that country could do was keep him

13

or her in underwear — right? Later, I was also appalled to read of widely publicized scandals at U.S. military facilities: life-threatening mold at Walter Reed Hospital, tragic delays in treatment at VA hospitals, troops and their families living in unsanitary, unhealthy housing and on food stamps. When you think of people serving and protecting America, think diplomats, and think also of our military. As someone who was protected by Marine Security Guards around the world, thank you and — Semper Fi.

T/F: A diplomat is "a man (more on that bias later!) sent abroad to lie for the good of his country." I never had to lie for my country, but . . .

At the U.S. Embassy in Kiev I worked on the 1994 U.S.-Russia-Ukraine Trilateral Statement in which the United States and Russia agreed to ensure Ukrainian security if Ukraine gave up its nuclear weapons.[2] By 1996, Ukraine had given up almost 2,000 nuclear warheads and weapons. By 2014, Ukraine had respected this agreement for 18 years, but Russia invaded Ukraine and today is still occupying Crimea and other sovereign Ukrainian territory.[3] U.S. security assurances as Ukrainians fought and died to defend their country were, at a minimum, not reassuring. Were our assurances a lie?

Credibility counts. Failing to honor our word has serious implications. If we can't be trusted, alliances and agreements to protect peace and promote prosperity will not happen. Worse, if our allies know we can't be counted upon, will we be able to depend on them when *we need them?* In 2019, the President of the United States withheld almost $400 million in military assistance funding for Ukraine at a time when Ukrainians were fighting and dying to repel Russian invaders. Integrity is a critical component of international agreements without which security, peace and prosperity are impossible. In 2020, the independent, nonpartisan Government Accountability Office (GAO) that ensures the integrity of U.S. government activities declared that withholding these funds was illegal.[4]

T/F: A diplomat is (paraphrasing various quotes) "a person who can tell you to go to hell and make you think you're enjoying the ride!"

This is an exaggeration, but it is the business of diplomacy to influence people and nations to work towards a common good. It's difficult to get people to act against their self-interests. But in the face of the awful destruction of war, or the damage secrecy, lies and corruption can do to civil society, it is possible to convince people that democracy, openness and rule of law are in their best interest and worth working towards. This message was particularly powerful after the fall of the Soviet Union, when the picture of a prosperous and free United States was worth thousands of words.

T/F: Diplomats are "unelected bureaucrats." This is true, and has been for over a hundred years. In the 1800s, the patronage or "spoils" system was pervasive in government in the United States. The winning party in any election gave government jobs to its supporters to reward their loyalty and ensure future victories. Integrity and job competency were irrelevant. When President James Garfield was assassinated in 1881 by a disgruntled officer-seeker, calls for reform spread and in 1883 the Pendleton Act created the *apolitical, merit-based system* the United States has today.[5] In 1939, the Hatch Act was passed which strengthened this separation of civil service from partisan politics.[6] Further, the 1978 Ethics in Government Act enforces ethics in the U.S. government by requiring U.S.

government personnel — including politicians and political appointees — to provide comprehensive financial disclosure information.[7] Finally, and specific to the Foreign Service, the 1924 Rogers Act called for competitive entry examinations for Foreign Service Officers to "attract and retain the best [diplomats]. . . " and require that promotions be merit-based.[8]

Today, the Association for Diplomatic Studies & Training, a repository of historical information on the U.S. Foreign Service, notes that "of the approximately 20,000 people who take the Foreign Service Officer Training Test each year, only about 500-700 are actually offered positions in the Foreign Service."[9] The rigorous exam — along with the security and other screening required — ensures that only the best are selected to represent the United States abroad. Diplomats are also evaluated annually in a competitive "up-or-out" promotion system. They must continue to excel, while complying with all ethical, security and professional requirements noted above, or leave the Foreign Service. Diplomats may be disciplined, fired, or even jailed for ethical violations or for failure to capably execute their responsibilities.

There is, however, another type of "un-elected bureaucrat" in government today, the political appointee who is personally appointed to government positions by the president. The Trump Administration's political appointees are frequently in the news for ethical, professional and security violations.[10] Some have been let go, but screening and accountability must improve and the President should set the standard for ethical professionalism. The United States deserves — and needs — a better caliber of public servant for its national security. The U.S. Government has taken serious steps over the past century to avoid the corruption and dysfunction that political favoritism in government causes. We do not need a return to the "spoils" system.[11]

T/F: Diplomats are "disloyal." False, but this untruth has also been around for some time.

- First, diplomats and other federal employees swear an oath to support and defend *the Constitution,* not to support any individual or political party.[12] Diplomats may be Republicans, Democrats, or independent. They may not practice politics or support one party over another in the course of their official duties as diplomats, but they must support and defend the Constitution.

- Second, it is a diplomat's responsibility to "speak truth to power," although they often do so at great risk to their career. In the the 1950's Senator Joseph McCarthy campaigned, based on unsubstantiated rumors and allegations, to expose what he claimed was the communist infiltration of American government. The Department of State's "China Hands" were particular targets, blamed for "losing China to the communists" since they reported the unwelcome but accurate news that the Chinese Communists would probably defeat the Chinese Nationalists. The Nationalists did lose and fled to Taiwan. One officer fired at that time (John Patton Davies) was only exonerated 15 years later.[13]

Fast forward to 2019. Experts from different agencies with decades of service *in both Republican and Democratic administrations* properly brought what they determined was significant information to their superiors. They followed official policy and procedure, yet were publicly attacked by the President, vilified in social media, and some even lost their jobs for doing their sworn duty. Specifically, they brought their concerns to their superiors about the highly unusual stoppage of authorized funding to Ukraine. We don't need a return to the ugliness of the McCarthy era during which allegations counted as truth, truths were buried, and a demand for bogus "loyalty oaths" were used to end careers and ruin lives.

The independent nonprofit Center for Public Integrity investigates issues that it believes betray the public trust (which is to say, you and me) and the public record the Center compiled of the Ukrainian funding timeline history is damning. Bribery is an illegal or unethical offering to influence the recipients' actions. In the Ukrainian context, President Trump held up almost $400 million in duly authorized critical military aid unless Ukraine agreed to "do a favor" and investigate a political opponent. As noted previously, the Government Accountability Office determined that the White House broke the law by withholding this aid. The White House also ignored subpoenas, blocked witnesses, and tried to illegally identify the whistle-blower even after independent witnesses publicly confirmed the whistleblower's information.[14]

Returning to the basic question, is it disloyal to present information on our government, including on possible illegal activity, to the American people? Personally, I want to know what my government is doing, but I recognize this is a fine balancing act. Federal law protects whistleblowers who work *through appropriate channels* to encourage transparency and accountability. But there have been leaks, such as WikiLeaks, that do not go through proper channels, but provide classified intelligence directly to the media. These leaks have had a chilling effect on U.S. diplomats ability to obtain critical information as our international contacts no longer trust us to protect them and their information.

T/F: Disagreement is still disloyal. Also false, but leaking internal deliberations is unprofessional and diplomats who do so can be penalized.

The State Department has an official Dissent Channel that was initiated in 1971 when diplomats worried that constructive criticism and differing views on the Vietnam War were being suppressed.[15] The Dissent Channel provides diplomats with a forum for "...responsible dissenting and alternative views on substantive foreign policy issues . . ." The channel can bring critical information to policy makers so they have all the facts needed to make the best decisions possible. Dissent Channel cables are never anonymous, but are not for publication. Rather, they are for internal State Department deliberations only. Officers who respect the confidentiality of the Dissent Channel have protections from reprisals or retaliation for their dissenting views on policies and programs. Officers who leak these messages, however, can face legal penalties.[16]

Our nation was founded on dissent — rebellion against the tyranny of an English king, and *for*, among other things, freedom of speech. We honor as patriots men and women — from Nathan Hale, through Abraham Lincoln to Rosa Parks and Martin Luther King — who spoke out and even died to make this country better. While the Tories of 1776 and the white nationalists of today might disagree, a traitor is not, by definition "anyone who does not agree with them."

A note on "classifications" and particularly "secret" vs. "open source" information would be useful here. Today, when the Internet gives us access to satellite imagery of everything from our neighbor's back-yard barbecue to images of human rights atrocities, it is difficult to hide things. Yet some information remains secret, whether it be the true capabilities of Iranian nuclear programs, U.S.

government attempts to discover these capabilities — or U.S. government deliberations on what to do with information discovered. People who may be risking their lives to combat rogue governments as they work for nuclear safety and disarmament deserve the protection of secrecy. Information about American technological advances that help monitor Iranian compliance with international nuclear agreements, and that could help the Iranians avoid or circumvent such technology if made public, should also be protected.

Clearly, then, some information that helps ensures global safety and security should be classified, according to carefully vetted guidance. Information on internal policy deliberations should also be tightly held. Think of the business world: if you can't protect trade secrets, you can't protect your business. The business of government is governing. Classifying information can be appropriate. Using classifications to protect errors, egos and downright lies, however, is abuse. Whistleblowing is the well-considered, judicious process to bring information to appropriate authorities through protected channels to determine if classifications are being handled properly.

WikiLeaks, which notoriously released troves of classified information, is not an example of whistleblowing, but rather individuals acting arbitrarily as judge, juror and potentially as executioner, outside of protected channels and with no concern about consequences. It is clear that informants who used to provide American government officials with information essential to protecting American troops and other interests across the globe now hesitate to talk to us for fear of disclosure. Personally, I would be interested to know if WikiLeaks resulted in harm or death to anyone who has provided such information to American officials.

T/F: Diplomacy is expensive. Well, let's talk about the "dollars and sense" of diplomacy. In 2016, Secretary of State John Kerry noted that most Americans incorrectly believe that foreign aid accounts for about a quarter — or even a third — of the U.S. federal budget. In fact, diplomacy, including U.S. diplomatic facilities and all personnel, is usually about 2-3 cents per dollar of the discretionary (not including Social Security and other mandatory programs) cost of the federal budget.[17]

T/F: There are only about 8,000 Foreign Service Officers, and around 6,000 Foreign Service Specialists (Security, IT experts and others without whom we could not conduct diplomacy) worldwide.[18] Compare that to **1.3 million** active duty military[19] and more than 800,000 military reservists, and a 2019 Department of Defense budget of over $686 billion, or over half (50 cents per dollar) of the discretionary federal budget.[20]

Interestingly, a November 2019 *Economic Times* article notes that China now has more diplomatic missions (276) than the United States (273) does[21] — and I never saw a Chinese mission as understaffed as the many U.S. missions in which I worked. If we relinquish our world leadership to the Chinese, it should be a thoughtful considered decision, and not the result of thoughtless and short-sighted budget cuts.

Fact: In 2016, the Department of State, combined with the U.S. Agency for International Development, had a total budget of $50.3 billion.[22] In December of that same year, the *Washington Post* reported on a Pentagon study that identified $125 billion in potential savings from the military budget over five years through streamlining its bureaucracy, better use of technology and other measures.[23] In other words,

Pentagon savings over five years through better management could pay for about two and a half years of diplomacy. The military is critical to America's security, but must operate in conjunction with civilian partners. As former Defense Secretary James Mattis consistently emphasized throughout his military career:

"If the State Department isn't fully funded, then the military will need even more money, ultimately to buy more ammunition."[24]

Diplomats are a force multiplier of incalculable value, but let's calculate one. Leaving aside the wars diplomats have stopped, let's compare two Republican-Administration wars in the same region. In the 1990-1991 First Gulf War, the United States had a fact-based plan forged by military and diplomatic area experts who persuaded 38 allied nations to support the plan. This coalition got Iraq out of Kuwait for $61 billion, of which the United States paid about $7 billion. Our allies paid $54 billion and fought and died with us.[25]

Contrast that to 2003-2011 Second Gulf War, which had a bad plan, bad intelligence on alleged weapons of mass destruction, and almost no allies. The Congressional Research Service notes that this war cost the United States $784 billion, or over one hundred times the cost of the First Gulf War. Add in the cost of the incredible upheaval this war caused in the Middle East for which we're still paying, and it's clear that the forethought and diplomacy of the first Gulf War gained us a serious bargain.[26]

Finally, think about the Tbilisi embassy employee I mentioned in the acknowledgement, who volunteered to serve at the U.S. Embassy in Baghdad. The cost to the United States was much less than sending an officer, and the value was *priceless!* That kind of loyalty can't be bought or bombed into existence. Rather, the powerful draw of American ideals and the inspiring work of the people who embody those ideals and support and defend them gain us friends and allies. The work of diplomacy is unending, can be tedious, makes great demands on the practitioner and may not always pay off in the short-term. But the end results are well worth the effort.

Gardeners reading this will understand what I'm talking about because they know their plants, the environment in which the plants grow and the care and patience needed to tend them. They carefully cultivate their plants and hope for the best. As in diplomacy, though, storms, pests and other unexpected events can wreck even the most painstaking efforts, but that doesn't mean the work should not be done. Again, no test, but keep in mind the State Department's core mission statement: Diplomats work to create a more secure, democratic and prosperous world for the benefit of the American people and the international community.

So on to Timbuktu, and the start of my diplomatic adventures. And for those of you who would like maps and more on the many places to which I've travelled, I can highly recommend the CIA's World Factbook, National Geographic and Wikipedia websites.

3

AND SO BEGINS MY WILD RIDE
BAMAKO, MALI, 1988-1990

I must begin at the beginning though, and admit that this wild ride almost did not happen. After I took the "totally unbiased, merit-based" Foreign Service test, I received a notice that I had not passed the test. My scores in black and white on the notice, however were higher than the "passing score" mentioned in that same notice. I was never a math major, but I did think that if *my score was higher than the passing score, it should mean that I passed.*

At the time, I was a fairly new counterterrorism analyst working for the Department of State's Bureau of Diplomatic Security. Who was I to question the almighty and powerful Oz, sorry, government? Full disclosure: I am irreverent, but also an incurable optimist. I believe in truth, justice and the American way. Some weeks after receiving the notice, I finally got up the nerve to call the testing office to see if they might have made a mistake. The call was odd: no apologies, noticeable pressure to become a political officer rather than the management officer I wanted to be, and, finally, an admission that I had, indeed, passed. I was a bit miffed, so I asked — "Were you ever going to tell me I'd passed?" only to be met with dead silence.

Several years later, the light dawned. I was notified that I was part of a class action lawsuit filed by women in 1976 against the Department of State for gender discrimination.[27] For years, men who had scored lower on the Foreign Service test were admitted over women with higher scores so there would be "enough men" in the Service. Further, in the breakdown of the separate scores for political, consular, economic and management expertise, men were steered into "more prestigious" political positions and women into management and consular jobs — even if the women had scored higher than their male colleagues on political expertise. Women also were assigned to less-developed countries instead of to such countries as England and France, and were woefully underrepresented in senior diplomatic ranks including Ambassador.

The good news is that rule of law overcame tradition, and the blatant discrimination was stopped. Women won the lawsuit *in 1987*, although it wasn't until 2010 that the lawsuit was closed because the State Department had either ended its unfair practices or made sufficient progress towards meeting non-discrimination goals. Women were accepted into the Foreign Service if they passed the exam, were given equal opportunities to serve as political officers, in first world countries, and at senior levels if merited. In fact, the State Department had been slowly moving away from discriminatory practices for years. By the 1970s, women were no longer required to resign from the Foreign Service if they got married, which requirement had never applied to men. A practice that required the spouses of male Foreign Service Officers to serve at embassies as unpaid 'volunteers" — they were actually rated on how well they performed their duties on their husbands' official annual evaluations — was also stopped.

Overcoming this discrimination took years, but I compare that to the experience one local national staffer I knew had with her government. She was royalty and thus well connected, and her progressive parents had supported her study at a prestigious university abroad. After graduating with honors, she presented herself as "ready to serve" at her country's Foreign Ministry where they told her they would be more than happy to have her serve — tea! She came to work at the U.S. Embassy and both we and her country benefitted from her amazing intellect, hard work ethic, good sense and good humor.

One final comment before I get to my first tour, in Mali, West Africa, and to its most famous city, Timbuktu, twice! Many countries across the world share a similar New Year's superstition, that the way you start a new year is the way that new year will unfold. So make sure that midnight kiss is with someone special, fill your wallet to ensure prosperity, clean your home for a clean and fresh new start . . . you get the idea. Replace "New Year" with "career" for this superstition and eerily enough, the same goes. My instructor for my Foreign Service orientation class talked about an officer who started his career in a coup, and then encountered coups forever afterwards. So he was sent to Fiji — a beautiful South Pacific paradise — for a bit of a break. Fiji had a coup shortly after his arrival, and the joke became that the U.S. government should send him to Moscow as a secret weapon to end the Cold War. My career had multiple, but enduring themes: chaos countered by creativity, tech troubles everywhere, and long, grueling work hours but with great people and major accomplishments. It was an incredible experience that was sometimes scary, but also tempered with humor and good fun. I have no regrets, and hope that you'll enjoying sharing my adventures.

All Foreign Service Officers (FSOs) take a basic orientation class[P2-4], and some receive language or other supplemental training before their first assignment. My training time was short, as I already had the French needed for my assignment as well as a basic understanding of State Department policies and practices from my Civil Service experience as a counterterrorism analyst. In contrast, my flight to Bamako, Mali, in West Africa, seemed agonizingly long. I teared up thinking about the soul-searing isolation I could expect in those pre-Internet days. I also teared up due to the whole range of shots I'd had for protection for everything from typhoid, tetanus and smallpox to yellow fever. The worst was the gamma globulin shot. It left rear ends sore for days and was always administered, for some reason, shortly before interminably long plane rides that made sitting an issue.

Isolation in Mali was real. Mali is a landlocked country, with its northern city of Timbuktu at the edge of the great Sahara desert. The Malian national capital had only one "safe" flight out per week, phone calls could cost almost $5/minute (real money in those days), and the Internet was non-existent. But then I landed in Bamako and was met by a cheerful embassy employee who helped me through the crowded and chaotic airport, and my American embassy sponsor, both of whom made me feel so welcome. I still remember my first delicious African meal of chicken in peanut sauce followed by that American staple — carrot cake — in the mix of Mali and America that colored my tour and made it so enjoyable.

Back in the United States we had reliable running water.

In Mali, we sat around my swimming pool, my water reservoir for the many times I had no water. In Ohio, I had electricity, light and air conditioning. In Bamako, we sat poolside under some shade trees my first day, as a power outage and generator trouble meant that my house was too hot to stay inside. But as my new colleague, my sponsor and I discussed family, home towns, who's who, things to see and do, work and play . . . I felt right at home in this discussion that could easily have been held in my hometown of North Canton, Ohio. Fortunately, an embassy technician came to fix my generator, so I soon had electricity, light and even air conditioning.

I have less fond memories of boiling and lightly bleaching my water and then soaking vegetables and fruits in it, but still loved that other American staple done Malian style — wonderful strawberries, slightly mushy from that required soaking and rinsing. In another mash-up of cultures, I learned that neighbors would happily loan me cooking gas, particularly when I ran out of gas in the middle of cooking for guests. For me, this was the Ohio equivalent of stepping next door to borrow a cup of sugar.

Mali's remoteness and the lack of reliable transportation[P5 & P8], including out of the country, led to scary incidents. An American with cerebral malaria had to wait for days until the plane out of town to western medical care arrived. The rumor at the embassy was that our ambassador parked in front of the plane until the pilot agreed to let this gravely ill person board. Airmail took weeks to arrive, and as a "newbie," I was afraid my credit union was going to repossess my car after it notified me that "I hadn't filled out the proper paperwork prior to shipping it overseas." Never mind that I'd filled out and had personally hand-delivered this paperwork before I'd left. My more experienced boss assured me that the credit union was unlikely to come to Africa to collect. And in the ambassador's first call to Washington almost two weeks after the central telephone exchange broke down (not a terrorist attack, just years of poor maintenance), Washington was startled to learn that we'd been out of contact. Headquarters hadn't noticed the lapse in communications.

But where's the exotic, you ask? Where are the desert nomads riding their camels into the sunset? Thanks to my wonderful ambassador, I soon had the opportunity to travel to Djenne and Segou. Seeing Djenne, a United Nations Educational, Scientific and Cultural (UNESCO) World Heritage Center with its famous mosque, and Segou, which was once the capital city of an African empire, was amazing.[P6-7] The architecture was awesome, the desert, stark but beautiful — and the people were kind, creative, thoughtful fishermen, farmers, artisans and others treasuring and celebrating their homes, their families and their marvelous, millennia-old culture.

By the time I got to the mysterious and beyond-the-ends of-the earth Timbuktu via a days-long journey up the Niger river,[P6-7] I'd given up searching for the exotic and just enjoyed the culture and cuisine, people and beauty of this ancient city. Even when I went into the desert outside Timbuktu, hospitable villagers brought out their precious sealed water bottles (so we less hardy city folk wouldn't get sick), as well as the nicest feast they could offer with the best seats in the house.

I saw striking differences — and similarities — to Europe, which I knew from my travels and studies as a college student. I'd been to midnight mass at St. Peter's in Rome at Christmas, and I saw the same spirituality on an eerie, moonlit night in Timbuktu during the Muslim holy month of Ramadan. The men had gathered outside the mosque and were together reading aloud from the Koran — by the light of one bare bulb hanging haphazardly from the mosque's roof. I was transported back to the Middle Ages, with a twist: ancient religion, new-tech lighting and a spirituality for the ages.

Timbuktu is also a UNESCO World Heritage Site that was renowned in the 15th and 16th centuries as a center of a more moderate Islam, trade and scholarship. For anyone who has read or seen the movie *The Monuments Men* about saving the treasures of the western world from Nazi depredation, try *The Bad-Ass Librarians of Timbuktu*. Both tales tell the story of a few intrepid men who worked under dire circumstances to save irreplaceable treasures (in the latter case, of Islam) from thugs who would have destroyed them.

Many Malians I met were undeniably poor, but nevertheless had a rich life of family, friends, music and artisanry. They did not have the luxury of the "planned obsolescence throw-away" economy of the United States, but used, then re-used and then repurposed, anything they could get their hands on. Banking in Mali was different, too, than in the United States. I'd done my homework and read a lot on Africa including *Africa Adorned*, a beautiful full-color coffee-table book that paid homage to the jewelry of Africa. I was dismayed upon arrival in Africa, though, to see that most jewelry was plastic. It took me a few weeks to realize that due to years of drought, women had sold their wealth and no longer owned the beautiful jewelry I had expected to see. I was pleased, upon returning years later in more prosperous times, to see that women had "replenished their bank accounts" and were once again wearing glorious gold works of art.

So what did I do for the United States during my two

years in Bamako? I was not the political officer most familiar to many Americans, and did not write a treaty, stop a war or do things that are so often captured in stories of the Foreign Service. But as a management officer I kept the embassy running and even made it better. Back in 1989, I helped set up some of the first unclassified computers at the mission, and supported one incredibly bright Malian in his bid to become our computer manager. He needed no help on tech, but I did accompany him on one of his first troubleshooting calls to a rather grouchy senior embassy officer. I quickly realized why the officer's "new tech" computer wasn't working — it wasn't plugged in. I spent a few moments on "diagnostics," then let him know "it was a loose connection and that we'd be happy to return if the problem reoccured." We saved the officer's face and enjoyed a laugh once out of earshot. My former warehouseman later became a highly regarded roving tech troubleshooter for the State Department covering all of Africa. Not coincidentally, this was a much cheaper option than sending a team out from Washington to fix problems.

Tech was a boon and a bane for many of my tours. In Mali, I was pleased to read the glowing evaluation my boss gave me after my first year at post. He copied it onto a floppy disk (a plastic disc about the size of a saucer that was used to save and transfer documents from one computer to another in the early days of computers) and gave it to me for review. I was embarrassed to admit to my boss, after my short drive across town from the embassy to my office annex, that this floppy disc that I'd placed on my dashboard had melted down in the hot African sun. I asked him for another copy, and he graciously did *not* amend my evaluation to reflect that "this officer needs to be more cognizant of the work environment!"

Later, I served as the political officer for months after our seriously ill political officer was evacuated back to the United States. My first démarche (usually an "in-person" appeal to a host-country counterpart to influence the host country's policies or actions) was to ask to the Malian government to join with the United States on a United Nations vote against the proliferation of nuclear weapons. I conscientiously memorized my speaking points in French, had my navy blue "power suit" on, and had an official appointment with the senior level Malian who handled U.S. and U.N. issues.

Please note that Mali was a patriarchal, hierarchical society at the time, and age mattered. Further, many people shared a limited number of first and last names and family ties. Meanwhile, I was a young female officer who was temporarily replacing an older male officer. So when I showed up for my appointment at the Foreign Ministry, I was immediately sent off to see another young person in a poorly furnished area that reminded me of a small grade-school cafeteria.

Being the keen analytical observer diplomacy demands, I thought things did not look right for an important démarche, so I asked, "Are you Oumar, (the Malian equivalent of "John Smith"), minister for U.S. and U.N. Affairs?" And he said yes. So I introduced myself and went into my carefully-memorized talk, only to be asked "Are you American" and then told "you can speak English." That latter was a heart-stopper as I hadn't memorized my speech in English, but I gamely continued, translating in my head as rapidly as I could. After which, "Oumar" again questioned me "So why are you telling me this?" I thus discovered that I'd given my first démarche to Oumar the translator, who translated U.N. documents as needed. Oumar kindly accompanied me to his uncle the Minister to explain to him why I was now late for my meeting.

We all laughed, and my ambassador later commended my "great relations with everyone at the Foreign Ministry" in my annual personnel evaluation. I was never nervous going to the Foreign Ministry again, and always got the Malians to agree to take the actions we requested of them in these later démarches. I never, however, had the nerve to ask my ambassador if he had the full story on my first démarche.

My assignment to Mali was a wonderful introduction to the Foreign Service. Work was never dull, and ranged from traditional office work to travel upcountry to check on a water irrigation project, and even an official trip to Timbuktu to check on rumors of incipient extremist activity and drug and gun running. Travel to "work sites" could also be interesting, using everything from canoes and ferries to the defense attaché's plane.[P8]

This tour was not all work. I was able to travel extensively, played some tennis and softball, and even had a wonderful trip to Dakar in neighboring Senegal for an international softball tournament. That 600+ mile trip on the "Happy Bus" was unforgettable. Throw together some embassy and Peace Corps personnel (Americans and Malians), fill the bus with cheese doodles, m&ms, pop tarts and other junk food, and mix on a 14-hour ride. Everyone was feeling a sugar high, as junk food was not part of the normal Malian or Peace Corps volunteer food chain.

Traveling such distances across hundreds of miles of desert with no convenient gas stations had to be planned carefully. We made good time despite a rough road, with our intrepid ambassador's driver racing ahead and then braking for the bad sections in ample time for us to slow down behind him. At one juncture, our ambassador actually stopped his car to caucus with all the caravan drivers, alerting us to a memorable pothole that he thought was just a mile or so ahead. So we inched forward slowly for about ten minutes, and then sped up again thinking that maybe the infamous pothole had been filled in. I was sitting up front in the Happy Bus and happened to glance out the window just in time to see the ambassador's vehicle go flying. Our vehicle braked, but still hit this gaping hole with enough speed to send cheese doodles and people flying. Fortunately we only incurred one sprained wrist (unfortunately to one of our best players). We remained in awe of the ambassador who, on a 600+-mile trip across mainly featureless landscape was able to remember a pothole to within a few miles. My return trip in a private vehicle was uneventful, although my traveling companion told me after we'd safely returned to Bamako that we had made the trip with no spare tire.

Other amazing trips included one to the cliffs of Bandiagara and to an enthronement ceremony. The Dogon people and others had lived high in the Bandiagara cliffs that for centuries provided them protection against both invaders and flash floods. The enthronement ceremony for local royalty was a colorful pageant of local music, costumes and celebration. And a trip up the Niger was inspiring. I passed cities from Mali's glory days, and also saw small towns that lined the banks of the Niger river with their industrious and creative residents who used old traditions and new techniques to eke out a living in that narrow band of life-sustaining land between river and desert. I hope the pictures I've included in this book from this trip will serve for several thousand words.[P6-7]

I treasured my time in Mali and the people with whom I worked, While I will not normally name names in this book to protect the privacy of friends and colleagues, I will occasionally name ambassadors as they are public persons — and you can easily figure out who they are through online research. In Mali, I had the great good fortune and honor to serve with Ambassador Bob Pringle and his wife Barbara, who would have made a brilliant ambassador herself in more enlightened times. I also had great relations with the small American community in Bamako, as well as with diplomats from other embassies.

The relationships I developed helped nurture the mutual aid culture that served the embassy, foreign nationals and Malians so well in this isolated post. Late one night, for example, I was called by a Canadian embassy colleague alerting me to a plane crash near Timbuktu. No Americans were on board, but a number of Canadian tourists were, and one had died. One of my responsibilities as management officer was to ensure that we had what we needed at this isolated embassy, and this, sadly, included coffins. When my Canadian friend called to ask if we had a coffin, I ran out to the warehouse in the middle of the night with my warehouse manager, got the coffin loaded onto a truck and sent it over to the grateful Canadians. Throughout my career, I cultivated relationships with others and always tried to be a model American: kind and caring, hardworking and helpful, and with a creative "can-do" attitude to overcome any obstacle. These were critical to my success as a diplomat, supporting and furthering the Department of State's mission goals to create a more secure, democratic and prosperous world for the benefit of the American people and the global community.

I loved my first tour as a Foreign Service Officer, and learned important lessons that would serve me well throughout my career: 1) get out and see and do all you can; 2) relish the differences; and on the work front: 3) creativity and calm in any crisis are crucial. One intrepid diplomat needed to get the Embassy to handle a weekend emergency during the usual seasonal flooding, but he was on the wrong side of a washed-out bridge. So he walked down to the river, bargained with a fisherman and was carried by canoe across the flooded river to get to the office.

A diplomatic "tour" or assignment is usually 2-3 years long, although some specialized and hardship tours may be only one year long. Thus my Mali tour came to an end, and .... I moved on to my next assignment in Montreal, Canada!

4

BEMUSED IN THE BANLIEUE/SUBURBS
MONTREAL, CANADA, 1990-1992

Most diplomatic missions known as "embassies," are located in a country's capital city. In some countries, however, additional diplomatic missions called "consulates" are located in major cities outside the capital. The U.S. mission in Montreal was one such consulate. This was my most "normal" assignment, but still bewildering. You see, everyone allegedly spoke English (or French) in Montreal, a city just an hour's drive north of the U.S./Canada border, but I often had trouble "understanding the natives." This, despite being an English-speaker myself and having studied at and received a diploma in French Language and Culture from the Sorbonne in Paris. One French diplomat I knew never spoke French in public in Montreal. She claimed it incited the natives to also speak a "French" that she couldn't understand, and she figured that if she only spoke English she'd have an excuse for any confusion.

The French language (Quebecois) used in Montreal dates back to the seventeenth century when the French first arrived in Canada. It reflects that the Montréalais were isolated from France for centuries. Add to that the influence of indigenous languages and English, and Quebecois could be colorful and confusing.

Also disorienting was the mix of people that could have been found in any good-sized American city. They often wore American clothes thanks to trips across the border for outlet mall shopping, and had American accents from time spent at U.S. schools, universities, or just in warmer southern climes. Many Canadian "snowbirds" spent winter months in Florida to avoid sometimes brutal Canadian winters. But Canadians are undefinably different. And since undefinable means "not able to define" ... I'm not even going to try. They were delightful, and I loved my job, the country and its people. I also enjoyed being able to visit my brother in the U.S. military who was stationed in New York City and having friends and family come to visit me.

I served as a consular officer this tour, with one temporary duty assignment (TDY) to our two-person consulate in Quebec City. It was a fascinating time to be a consular officer. I interviewed applicants for and adjudicated immigrant (stepping stone to U.S. citizenship) visas as well as non-immigrant (tourist and other short-term) visas. I provided services to U.S. citizens, helping Americans in Canada with everything from passports to emergency assistance. On the visa side, technicalities for the immigrant "Green Card Visa Lottery" and the non-immigrant Visa Waiver programs were being ironed out, and new systems for enhancing visa security were being introduced. This tour was an extraordinary introduction to the bureaucratic and political mash-up that is U.S. government visa and immigration policy.

The "Green Card Visa Lottery," officially known as the Diversity Immigrant Visa Program[28] was established to increase immigration from countries with recently low immigration rates to the United States — *or from Northern Ireland*. Jokers noted that the "Green" in the Lottery stood for the Irish, as supported by Senators Patrick Moynihan and Ted Kennedy and Speaker of the House Tip O'Neil. At the Consulate, we also handled traditional immigrant visas, which were based on: the principles of family reunification (U.S. citizens could sponsor immediate family members); working for a prospective employer who couldn't find a U.S. citizen to fill a specific job (in healthcare, for example); and for refugees fleeing from persecution in their home countries.

Politics definitely impacted our work. Consular officers are required to vet potential immigrants' criminal and health records, and to determine their likelihood of becoming a public charge, i.e., their potential to need welfare or other public assistance. Many Irish Green Card Lottery winners were initially ineligible for immigrant visas because *they were living illegally in the United States, and thus had broken U.S. law*. The Irish-American lobby geared up, and this "indiscretion" was deemed insufficient to deny a person an immigrant visa.

Several months after this change in immigration law — and after I'd denied one particular applicant a visa — he was back in my office. As proof that he would not become a public charge, he produced his paycheck stubs from the company *in the United States to which he illegally returned after I first refused him*. But, he claimed, he hadn't reentered the United States illegally. He told his mother that he'd take her to a well-known restaurant just across the border for Mothers' Day. She drove that day and told this story to the U.S. Immigration Officer (who only questioned her as driver), not knowing that her son would ditch her at the restaurant and return to his job.

That was one loophole that was quickly closed thanks to feedback from me and numerous colleagues working along the Canadian and Mexican borders. Immigration law was changed to reflect that everyone in a vehicle who benefitted from a lie told to an immigration officer by anyone in the vehicle would be liable for the lie.

Most people I interviewed for immigrant visas were good people who had had faced violence and persecution in their home countries, or had waited patiently for years to immigrate to join their U.S. citizen family members. All just wanted better lives for themselves and their children. But there were always a few who were not willing to wait their turn and who didn't think the law should apply to them. One U.S. citizen decided to try to get an immigrant visa in Montreal for his son's new foreign wife, since he didn't want to wait the months it would take to get her the visa back in her home country. I explained that we couldn't help this daughter-in-law with no ties to Canada, and that the wait for immigrant visas in Canada was also long. I counseled the father-in-law, given his statements that he would just take her over the border himself, that this would be alien smuggling (i.e., breaking U.S. law), and could have serious consequences. Several hours later the nearest U.S. Immigration office called. The father-in-law was trying to claim he'd never been told that it was illegal to bring his son's new wife into the United States without undergoing the proper immigration procedures. The fact that he was stopped while trying to smuggle her into the United States in the trunk of his car clearly indicated otherwise. The new wife's passport showing that we had just denied her a tourist visa (due to her declared intent to immigrate) did not help his case. I do not know what happened to the father-in-law, but I do know the wife did not illegally enter into the United States that day.

A quick reminder, dear reader, that in order to enter the United States, most non-U.S. citizens must apply in person for a visa, whether for the immigrant visas mentioned above, or for tourist and other short-term, *non*-immigrant visas. For short-term visas, applicants are still vetted for criminal and terrorist activity, but the key to obtaining the short-term visas is proving to the satisfaction of the consular officer in a personal interview that they will respect the terms of their visas, and *not overstay their visit to the United States.*

The Visa Waiver Program,[29] introduced in 1986, let citizens of certain countries with strong records of not overstaying their short-term *non-immigrant* visas visit the United States without actual visas. The program specifically allowed *air travelers* with short-term, round-trip tickets to enter into the United States after a talk with an immigration officer at the airport of entry, thus avoiding the consular/visa application step entirely. The U.S. government saved the time, effort and money of processing visas for these good applicants, and law-abiding foreigners benefitted from a streamlined process. U.S. citizens traveling to countries that were approved for the Visa Waiver Program also benefitted. In the spirit of reciprocity, U.S. citizens did not need to apply for visas to travel these countries.

At the U.S. Consulate in Montreal, it only took a few weeks of tour buses and cruise ships loaded with hundreds of tourists unexpectedly dropping by for visas to "just pop over the land border into the United States from Canada" to realize that this new program needed a tweak. After our feedback, Washington acted quickly to save us from these overwhelming floods of consular applicants while still ensuring the rigorous application of the Visa Waiver Program by adding a *land border crossing* provision to it.

Even after the tourist flood stopped, visa issuance was

challenging at this bustling border post. We saw thousands of applicants weekly: immigrants from many other countries who were now legal residents in Canada as well as visitors to Canada from dozens of countries who decided last minute to see Niagara Falls, or Disney Land — or in one interesting case, a polka competition.

Those few applicants who tried to "game the system" could be entertaining. We had one applicant come in every few months to play the sympathy card, claiming he had to get to New York for his mother's funeral. I met him on his third such attempt, and asked him politely just how many mothers he had. We — and immigration officers — always had to be alert to attempted visa fraud and we happily swapped stories from the front lines.

One memorable tale involved a seriously ill foreigner whose brother was a legal Canadian permanent resident. The sick man moved to Canada to take advantage of his brother's access to Canada's good, inexpensive health care — but then died. The family feared the Canadian authorities might figure out that the dead man had been receiving Canadian health care to which he was not entitled. To compound illegalities, they decided to use the live brother's legitimate access to the United States to fly the dead man out of Canada. As the dead man was wheeled around the airport, the family insisted that he was "just heavily medicated." But an airline employee recognized that it was a bit more serious than that, and the fraud quickly unraveled.

American Citizen Services was busy, but not quite as chaotic as visa services. I visited prisons to ensure incarcerated Americans were treated fairly, and fielded numerous complaints by Canadians that Americans were refusing to be repatriated to serve their sentences in the United States since "Canadian prisons were nicer." One weekend I met a flight that included Americans evacuated from the Middle East to make sure they were met by family members or other assistance. In another instance, I worked with a local charity to provide support for a family devastated by the loss of family members in a vacation tragedy. Fortunately, Canada and its institutions were well set up to handle deaths of Americans in their country with quick efficiency, coupled with kindness and empathy.

I also sat in on several court cases to ensure due process for Americans. One high profile case involved Mohawk Indians (one of whom had U.S. citizenship) who participated in a protest against plans to turn their sacred burial grounds in Oka, Quebec, into a golf course.[30] Tensions escalated, and a policeman was killed. The trial introduced me to Quebec Law based on the French Napoleonic Code as opposed to the British Common Law which ruled in the rest of Canada. Interestingly, there was a federal judge from Ottawa (the Canadian capital) in court to ensure due process despite the different legal system. I liked his opening statement that "the agency with the greater power has an ensuing greater responsibility to ensure that its power is not abused." He was emphasizing that the court had to provide translation (in both the Mohawk language and English), despite the high cost of the service, so the non-French speaking defendants could understand their own trial.

While I was not present at the conclusion of the trial, I can report that the golf course expansion on sacred grounds was cancelled, and the Canadian government later purchased the land to avoid future issues. At least one of the defendants served time, but the prominent public protests brought attention to a number of indigenous issues in Canada and people began to address them.

Then there was the penniless American trucker who ran

out of gas just a few miles from his home — on the wrong side of the border. He called the Consulate for help, and I told him to ask around to see if he couldn't get someone to give him a few bucks for the gas to get back home. I strongly emphasized that for any U.S. government loan, he'd have to fill out paperwork galore and could have problems if he didn't repay the loan as required. So he cadged a few bucks, got some gas — and driving north, not south — showed up an hour later at the consulate for a loan of about $15. There were also the three teenagers from New York who came up to Montreal to party in "lower-minimum-drinking-age Quebec." The three got so drunk that two drove home without the third, who showed up at the Consulate seeking assistance after spending the night on a park bench. Fortunately his embarrassed friends agreed to come back (sober) to pick him up.

Technology, as in Mali, was again troublesome. To help prevent the counterfeiting of U.S. visas, a special "visa foil" was superimposed on each visa. A program to reconcile the number of visa foils used with the number of visas issued was supposed to ensure secure visa processing through automation. I and my colleagues, however, spent countless unpaid overtime hours manually reconciling the hundreds of foil seals used each day with the number of visas issued as the automated program's numbers never matched up in its early days. The glitch in the reconciliation app was finally fixed; years later junior officers became eligible for overtime pay (which not coincidentally greatly reduced the "critical" overtime hours that these officers were required to work); and I bonded with one of my colleagues-in-counting so well that decades later she is still my BFF.

My temporary assignments during this tour included one to Quebec City and another covering a vacant management officer position in Montreal while I still carried out my regular duties. "Do more with less" and "do double or triple duty" was a recurring theme of my Foreign Service career. Incredible personnel and resource shortages became the norm after the fall of the Soviet Union and the State Department opened up 13 new embassies there with no additional personnel or funding for them. The impact was world-wide as people and resources from existing posts were diverted to these new posts, and the State Department suffered from these shortages for years. But at this key moment in history, everyone was excited and eager to work the long hours needed to take advantage of the end of the Cold War, and to create a more secure, democratic and prosperous world.

As a temporary duty management officer, one of my significant accomplishments was successfully overseeing the destruction of thousands of old consular files containing people's sensitive, private information. Remember, applicants had to provide financial information to prove they would not become a public charge, criminal records to prove they weren't felons and medical and other records. My oversight of this huge exercise occurred just a few short weeks before a Canadian government office became infamous for dumping confidential files curbside for regular trash pick-up. Journalists discovered the files, and local newspapers ran a story that was extremely embarrassing to the government.

Serving in Quebec City was fascinating as this was a two-person "we do it all" post. I simultaneously served as political, economic and management officers, and was even officially "in charge of the mission" when my boss was called back to Washington for consultations. I also continued with my visa work, which was interesting for the number of visa applicants I saw who thought they'd come to this smaller, less-assembly-line mission for "an easier visa." More than a few red faces resulted as I again denied applicants the visas I had previously denied them in Montreal. My only regret was that, despite having processed literally thousands of visas, I never met the hockey player, artist or other famous personality that many of my colleagues did.

Montreal was great introduction to consular affairs, and wonderful for everything else. I took classes at McGill University, and delighted in the cuisines, arts and cultural mosaic that are integral to Canada. I made new friends and had old friends and family come to visit, including all three of my brothers, one of two sisters and my mom. It was a pleasure sharing with them the international jazz, ballet, film, fireworks, winter carnival and other festivals for which Montreal is so well-known. I even got to see the Cirque du Soleil practicing as I passed their facility near my neighborhood.

But every assignment must end, and so on to the wild west, even if technically I was headed east — to the former Soviet Republic but now-newly-independent Ukraine.

5

THE WILD, WILD — EAST
KIEV, UKRAINE, 1993-1995

My next assignment was to Ukraine, via ten months of Ukrainian training at the Foreign Service Institute's (FSI) School of Language Studies. My experiences there foreshadowed the craziness to come in Ukraine, my "wildest" assignment. Most officers get a short course on a country's history, culture, current events and key issues before going to a new post so they can be a credit to the United States and do their job well. Additionally, if the Department determines that an officer needs the local language to do his or her job, that officer will get anywhere from a couple of weeks to up to 2 years (for Arabic or Chinese, for example) of language training. Officers who already speak a language get preference on assignments that need the local language, saving the Department time and money.

I used my French in Mali and Canada but had no Ukrainian. Meanwhile, the U.S. government was sending a strong signal to Ukraine and the other new countries of the former Soviet Union that it respected them as independent countries with their own unique languages and cultures. This was particularly important in Ukraine, where Ukrainian had been suppressed for decades and speaking it was a source of national pride. Decades of suppression made it difficult to find modern language training materials: my textbook dated to the 1950s, and I still remember the quaint terminology of its first chapter, on "pigs and chickens on the collective farm." Alternatively, we had access to poems from the esteemed nineteenth century Ukrainian poet and writer Taras Shevchenko. Neither helped me much with my language studies, but Ukrainians appreciated that I knew a little about their revered hero who was exiled in Czarist Russia for his writings in Ukrainian and for promoting Ukrainian independence

Before the Internet and online shopping, it took me weeks just to find woefully outdated English-Ukrainian and Ukrainian-English dictionaries. I used them to prepare oral presentations for class, only to be asked by the teacher "where did you get that word" or have him tell me "we don't use that word," or "that word doesn't mean what you think it does." Who knew that carefully "*un*-memorizing" words would be a part of language training! Totally frustrated, I proposed a visit to the Ukrainian Embassy to get some decent material. The embassy was so new that my instructor and I meandered through a construction site and surprised the Ukrainian ambassador in his not-yet-finished office. He was gracious, though, and we were supplied with embassy press releases in Ukrainian from then on.

More difficulties arose from the language training's focus (apart from chickens, pigs and poetry) on preparing political and economic officers for their duties. Older, more established language programs at FSI included vocabulary appropriate to consular duties (births, deaths, overstaying

visas), but few programs had the terms useful to procurement, leasing, repair and maintenance that I would need
as a "General Services" Officer trying to help the embassy
function. So my highly politicized vocabulary-adapt-
ed-to-daily-life got some odd looks. One day at the embassy
we almost had a generator overload. I yelled "demobilize"
the generator — the closest I could come to "shut it down
now!" — and the generator was shut down before it melted
down. Some local staff were sure I was CIA. I didn't help
matters by wearing a bright blue beret — the same color as
Russia's Spetsnaz (Special Forces) — when I was posted to
Kiev's airport to support President Bill Clinton's first official
visit to Ukraine.[P9]

But it was a point of honor to speak Ukrainian with
Ukrainians, and they were patient with my efforts. On official visits to Ukrainian counterparts, I often smiled to see
Ukrainian textbooks and dictionaries in their offices that
showed that they were working to perfect their national
language. Many Ukrainians grew up speaking only Russian,
or if they knew Ukrainian, never knew enough — or were
permitted to use it — at work. Over a century after Taras
Shevchecnko was convicted of the crime of using Ukrainian
and exiled by the czars, Ukrainians who used their own
language could still get into trouble under the Soviets. In
newly independent Ukraine, my ability to speak Ukrainian,
and the fact that the U.S. government honored Ukraine
by taking the time and money to teach it to me, won the
United States friends and helped me succeed in my job. In
addition to the political value, I didn't take twice the time
to accomplish even the most simple tasks by having to run
everything through an interpreter in a country where very
few people spoke any English at the time.

So in 1993, just two years after Ukrainian independence

from the Soviet Union, I arrived in Kiev as the General Services Officer, tasked with finding the people, places (housing and offices) and things (everything from office supplies to vehicles for embassy use) needed to maintain, operate and expand the U.S. embassy there. During my two years working in Kiev, the embassy almost *tripled* in size, from 30 to 90 American diplomats, and to almost 300 local Ukrainian staff. My colleagues helped Ukraine develop basic democratic institutions, supported its rule of law and efforts to reduce crime and corruption, and *removed all nuclear weapons from Ukraine within two years* — and I was going to do the best job possible to ensure that they had what they needed to do theirs.

Ukraine was dealing with an existential question — go pro-Russian or pro-West? More fundamentally, it had to deal with elections. People were in shock after the 1994 presidential election: they had thrown out the Russian-communist-supported incumbent Leonid Kravchuck for a more western-leaning Leonid Kuchma — legally, and without military intervention. Celebrations came days later after they recovered from the shock, and continued as the new president declared an anti-corruption campaign. In just one example, the few Ukrainians I knew who had cars (and were thus considered "rich") happily reported that police no longer stopped them for the bribe money they usually demanded to augment their pitifully low salaries and enable them to survive.

Ukraine also had to build a new democracy from the ground up, from fighting the corruption of the old regime through enacting and implementing new laws and establishing a new currency. It also had to develop new supply chains for everything from fuel and food to toilet paper — and legacy supply chains from the former Soviet Union weren't too good to begin with. Jokes about swimsuits in September and snow shovels in July were founded on fact, and neither snow shovels nor swimsuits were worth the long waits people endured to finally purchase them.

The American political wrinkle in this assignment was setting up Embassy Kiev — and a dozen other new posts across the former Soviet Union — *with no **new** resources and no **new** staff* for the State Department. Funding and staff were taken from existing posts with no decrease in their workloads, to the detriment of all U.S. missions worldwide. This exercise caused serious staffing gaps and other negative consequences that hurt the United States strategic and foreign affairs interests for years.

Former Secretary of State John Kerry once said that Americans believe that foreign aid counts for a quarter to a third of the US federal budget, or 25-30 cents for each dollar.[31] This myth persists today, although (you did read Chapter 1, right?), it is and has historically been much closer to under three cents per dollar. It was in part a response to the myth that the State Department was the fat in the federal budget — and was allegedly mismanaging it too — that the State Department claimed that it could capably open the 13 new posts with existing resources.

U.S. diplomats worldwide worked long, hard hours to offset the staffing shortages and advance U.S. interests in those exciting times: the Berlin Wall had fallen and we had "won the Cold War." In Ukraine, we were particularly eager to help bring freedom, peace, prosperity and other benefits of democracy to Ukrainians who had suffered so long under Soviet rule. Unfortunately, the decision to move ahead without adequate resources handicapped our efforts and U.S. efforts worldwide. It took years before the State Department's resources began to catch up to its needs.

Today, it's déjà vu all over again as State Department funding is being cut to the bone despite a wealth of issues demanding U.S. government attention — while China and Russia are supplanting American leadership across the globe.

Ukrainian political wrinkles included unpredictable laws. I dealt with old Soviet laws, Rada (Ukrainian parliamentary) rulings, and random presidential decrees (think "tweets!"). At any given moment as I tried to rent, buy or build, and furnish safe, decent housing for new employees who were arriving weekly, I felt I was being received as either the brave new spirit of entrepreneurial capitalism — or as a black-market speculator potentially undermining the Ukrainian soul. Americans, Canadians and other business men and women I knew were good sources of information on which laws prevailed and when, because they could be fined, jailed, or even be expelled from the country if they did not keep abreast of constantly changing rules and regulations. I frequently informed the embassy's senior political and economic officers on everything from changes in laws to changes in fuel and commodity prices.

Even without the political "wrinkles," daily life was tough. Ukraine lacked almost everything at the time, and what it did have was not the best quality, a particular concern as I tried to find housing for my colleagues. I didn't have my own place for weeks, but bunked with a first-tour officer I'd met in Ukrainian language training. Remember — I was the officer tasked with finding everyone housing, which included my own.

My delightful hostess surprised me with a dinner upon my arrival, and yes, you may make chicken Kiev jokes here. The bird she had proudly bargained for at the local market was clearly a Chernobyl[32] chicken, with odd body parts and an unbelievable toughness. This despite its "official health certification" that it was not radioactive. In Kiev just eight years after and about 60 miles away from the Chernobyl nuclear accident, "radiation-free" certifications were a dime a dozen and had zero credibility. Fortunately, my hostess had taken full advantage of her "consumables" shipment, a U.S. government-authorized shipment of canned groceries and other supplies to places where these things didn't always exist. Her shipment consisted mainly of chocolate and movies, and she generously shared both with me.

A late-night phone call as we were eating chocolate and watching movies showcased the harassment that U.S. diplomats could face, as well as well as my colleague's creativity in handling it. These calls, in a country where not everyone had a phone and all calls could be expected to be monitored, were a trademark of the former Soviet (KGB) and now Russian secret police. Unfortunately, some relics from the KGB remained in the new Ukrainian security service. In Moscow, colleagues offered guidance on handling these calls that included "don't blast an air-horn into the receiver or you'll wake up the next day to find your tires slashed." My hostess handled the problem differently: When the caller asked if Ivan was home, she babbled on in Russian for about 15 minutes with an off-the cuff soap opera saga about Ivan … hadn't you heard, he got a job with an international company, went abroad, his girlfriend was going to join him but then had an affair with his best friend but then they got together again . . . you get the idea. The KGB couldn't get a word in edgewise — and my friend was never again bothered by the midnight calls. Her spiel was even better than that night's movie and decadent dark chocolate!

Food and finding it ruled our daily lives. When I arrived, the corruption of the old regime still held sway, organized crime was a major concern, and the poor supply lines of the old Soviet system were severely disrupted. So even eating, let alone healthy eating, was a challenge. I defer to the medical experts as to whether a chocolate diet was healthier long-term than a radioactive food diet, or how my personal staples — canned high-sodium prepared foods, Snickers bars and cinnamon-frosted pop tarts measured up. At the embassy, lunch ladies produced sandwiches, candy, and other edibles out of the back of their car in a stealthy approach to avoid the risk of being robbed. Around town, one colleague joked about the ubiquitous liquid (vodka) diet coupled with a dearth of bathrooms for women at the various ministries. Paraphrasing patriot Nathan Hale, she "regretted that she had but one pair of kidneys to give for the sake of [her] country." Not drinking the vodka offered or not participating in the frequent toasts would have been rude beyond mention. Anyone fortunate enough to get authentic Ukrainian cuisine in this bread-basket of the former Soviet Union, however, enjoyed a real treat.

Things did get better. When I arrived in 1993, grocery stores had limited supplies, and if you needed milk only eggs were available — and vice versa. I felt like a survivalist with my stores of powdered milk, powdered eggs, canned soups, and pop tarts. The difficulties of moving from a centralized command to market economy and the "worship of the almighty dollar" occasionally worked in my favor though — bottles of lovely champagne and tins of caviar for a dollar made great hostess gifts. Gorgeous bouquets and long taxi rides (yes, in death traps, but sometimes unavoidable) were also cheap. Occasionally things cost even less than a dollar and vendors insisted on giving you change. Coins were unheard of, so hard candies served as change. I liked the red ones, but so apparently did all their other customers as cashiers tried to get me to accept orange or yellow candies instead. By the end of my tour in 1995 you could buy almost anything — at premium prices — as several imported goods stores had opened. Given that the imports could be from anywhere, knowing numerous foreign languages (from Arabic to Chinese) helped, or you just went with supper surprise.

Eating out was unpredictable, even towards the end of my tour. "Making dinner reservations" in the Ukrainian context often meant calling ahead to let owners know how many people were coming, and accepting whatever was on the menu of the day. By the end of my tour things were much better, and I eagerly drove to my favorite restaurant with family visitors to treat them to an authentic Ukrainian meal without calling ahead. Silly me. I was told that the restaurant didn't have enough food to feed four unexpected customers, so we all went back to my place for Campbell's soup. My sister graciously noted that this was a "special" cultural experience she hadn't had in years.

Then there was the wooden pizza. Towards the end of my tour, you could order pizza and other necessities of life and get them delivered. One brilliant but somewhat absent-minded colleague loved that pizza, but often forgot that he hadn't actually ordered any. So our creative IT techs, irked by the frequent disappearance of the pizza they ordered to sustain them through many late nights at the office, had my carpenters make them up a beautiful wooden pizza. They left it at the embassy entrance, and even our absent-minded officer got the message that he needed to start *ordering* the pizzas he was taking.

Living conditions were second after food as a key concern. Housing in the former Soviet Union was just one more not-so-good rationed commodity, and trying to find safe, basic housing was a trial. Electrical wiring didn't begin to approach U.S. safety code, and couldn't support the appliances that Americans considered standard. We managed to find some decent apartments — but the only play area for embassy children was its parking lot which glistened after rain with a beautiful, but certainly unhealthy, slick of oil and other contaminants. Simply breathing could be a chore. I sat outside on the balcony one nice fall evening. After about 20 minutes, I went inside to cough up copious black gunk that was a result of coal and wood-burning open fires and the leaded gas that were pervasive.

The invisible menace of radiation was an constant concern, and I worried that the embassy was not doing more to address it. Some of the first officers who arrived at post were issued radiation monitors, but I was astonished when one Temporary Duty Officer (TDYer) — stationed at the embassy for just a few short months — pulled his off his shirt and handed it to me saying "Here, you could probably use this." Frank was one smart officer who'd been pulled in to help get Embassy Kiev up and running, but clearly hadn't been given any guidance on this crucial tool — or if he had been, the guidance was unclear or had been forgotten in the press of urgent business and crises. In his months in Kiev, he had never turned it in to have it read, and hadn't kept track of potential radioactive sites he may have passed by. I immediately turned it in but never heard back on results. Fortunately, I was cultivating connections outside the embassy, and was able to get a good map of radioactive hot spots across Kiev from a German contact. I successfully used it for two years to get the least radioactive housing possible, but then came spring rains and flooding, totally altering the map. When I went back to my contact he indicated that he didn't know of any plans to do another study — but maybe the U.S. Embassy could do one? As far as I know the U.S. Embassy never did.

But we all persevered and made progress on supporting Ukraine's move towards democracy and the rule of law, the fight against corruption and the elimination of its nuclear arsenal. So on to work and the work site — literally a construction site — that was U.S. Embassy Kiev.

6

AT "THE OFFICE"
KIEV, UKRAINE - CONTINUED!

My first day on the job, I donned my navy blue "power suit" and heels and struck out for the embassy where I was introduced to the U.S. ambassador and my "office." The former was super, the latter — a tiny trailer I shared with three others, two computers, a copier and space heater. The heater was used by anyone who had to type up one of our innumerable cables or reports and thus needed to be able to take their gloves off in a trailer that was freezing during the long winter months. For a true understanding of the difference between Soviet and American thought, I give you the copier technician visit. This former Soviet was appalled at the trailer's freezing environment and chastised me for not providing a better, heated environment *for the copier*! Call me a decadent capitalist, but I would have been pleased with a better working environment for me and my colleagues.

Yes, call me a capitalist luxury lover, but I wasn't that excited about getting to the executive washroom (aka, the porta potty) that first day either, across a sea of mud that was the embassy construction site.[P10] Thankfully, we had sharp American guards supervising the construction site. After the debacle in the former Soviet Union in the 1980s, when U.S. Embassy Moscow was compromised by workers who infested the new construction with listening devices, these Cleared American Guards ensured that no bugs were planted or any other malicious activity occurred at U.S. Embassy Kiev. One of these alert guards saw my predicament (heels vs. mud), swept me into his arms, and gallantly carried me across to the porta potty. The next day I was still attired professionally, but had added indestructible hiking boots to my outfit.

I would have preferred not working in a construction zone, and probably lost a few years off my life the day a crane fell on my office trailer, denting its roof. Not-so-safe incidents at the embassy included the American who went out back for his usual smoke break and fell off the back of the building as the concrete porch he'd always lounged on was no longer there. Another officer's eyebrows grew back nicely after being singed when she unexpectedly walked into sparks flying from an arc welder. Fire was a constant hazard at both our homes and offices, but we fortunately had no injuries or loss of life.

Buildings directly adjacent to the U.S. Embassy also posed security concerns. During construction, women hung from their balconies propositioning the Cleared American Guards. Years later a Molotov cocktail was thrown into the embassy compound from one of those balconies.

For all the hardships I faced, Ukrainians faced many more hardships over which they had no control. We had generators, electricity, heat, plumbing, food, places to stay and other necessities of modern life. We could also get out of town, if needed. Ukrainians then often didn't have any of the above, and lived in a tough neighborhood to boot. The United States has Canada and Mexico as neighbors, while Ukraine has Russia and other countries that had invaded and pillaged Ukraine for centuries. Under Soviet rule from 1923-33 alone, millions of Ukrainians starved to death. The Ukrainians' small farms were combined into larger ones and food from these "collective farms" went to the State, and not to the people who worked on them.[33] Yet the Ukrainians I met were a proud people and were willing to work hard towards building the rule of law and to sustain their newly free and democratic country. Today, in 2020, Ukrainians are fighting and dying for their democracy and that freedom against the Russians who invaded their country in 2014 and continue to occupy sovereign Ukrainian territory. Remember Chapter Two and the US-Russia-Ukraine Trilateral Statement signed by the United States, Russia and Ukraine that was to protect Ukraine against such aggression?

But — back to the office. The embassy tripled in size to almost 400 people, including over 300 Ukrainians, on my watch. As General Services Officer, I drafted dozens of position descriptions, interviewed and hired people and then trained them to do their jobs before we could get to the normal work of a U.S. embassy. I also wrote dozens of annual evaluations that helped employees move into better and bigger jobs as we needed them. One remarkable employee started out as an "if it moves I've got it" facilitator. By the time I left two years later, we had seven people covering her original duties as travel agent, expediter, and procurement and shipping clerk. Moreover, she had helped to train and then supervised most of them.

Job interviews provided a fascinating window into Soviet life. One applicant carefully explained that she wasn't a slacker, but it took years for her to get her doctorate as she had to keep rewriting her dissertation — on a manual type-writer — to include the mandatory quotes from the leaders of the day: Brezhnev (1982), Andropov (1984), Chernenko (1985) and then Gorbachov. This was a *math* major, yet her dissertation had to pay homage to the political leaders of the day. Just one example of the waste of a government run by personality cult and personal connections versus a government run by civil service personnel selected and retained for their competency.

Bottom line, many people in Ukraine were conscientious and hardworking, but the system was not. In the former Soviet Union, the joke was, " You pretend to work, and we'll pretend to pay you." One instructor in my Ukrainian training shared a revealing story on Soviet window makers. The window-makers had a quota to meet and quotas were serious. But survival was even more serious, so a lot of raw material — and finished products — would "fall off the back of the truck." The creative window makers stretched their limited raw materials to make thinner and thinner windows and "ochen' zhal!", (too bad) if they all got to the stores or end-users broken or unusable. Quotas were met and the materials sold from the back of the truck enabled them to survive.

I treasure my samovar, the iconic Russian tea urn present in every local household, as one more example of this princi-ple. My samovar came from the historic Tula foundry, which was known for making cannon for Czar Peter the Great in the seventeenth century. Stories were told that even early on, workers at the foundry made samovars from "scrap" metal. Centuries later, the medallions stamped on my samo-var note that this "cannon factory" tea urn won a prestigious competition for artisanship. I love its beauty and the idea that it embodies of "turning swords into plowshares," or moving from military to peaceful productivity.

Under the Soviet system, employees were paid poorly, not always on time, and sometimes not at all. My warehouse manager made more working for the embassy than his former boss, the head of a scientific research institute. The poor salaries of the police, other civil servants and even judges were a key reason for Ukraine's endemic corruption. In contrast, U.S embassy Ukrainian personnel were paid in full and on time. The downside was that this made them lucrative targets for criminals on paydays. To protect my employees (in Ukraine and in several other countries), I worked with banks to develop and ensure access to such basics as reliable bank accounts and direct deposits. This also let them build equity and avoid the loan-shark loans they were used to. In one country I had to put a stop to a *bank's* attempt to rob our employees, pointing out that a 10% fee on each deposit "for the privilege" of using their bank was not acceptable.

Income tax issues proved problematic in Ukraine and several other countries I'd worked in, so the following is a montage of true stories taken from a number of them. Once direct deposits were ironed out, the next steps were *"your taxes are automatically deducted and directed to your government, which then responsibly uses this money for its citizens."* I helped establish systems for direct deposits, while my political and economic officer colleagues worked with the host country government to ensure the transparent and proper use of public funds. As representatives of the United States, we could not serve as tax collectors for a foreign government. I could, however, advise foreign governments and bank representatives and work with them to set up the systems that would make tax payment possible and verifiable.

U.S. diplomats don't pay taxes to the host country to which they are officially assigned, but we do pay U.S. taxes. Foreign national staff working at some embassies seemed to somehow believe they didn't need to pay local taxes — perhaps because sometimes there was no mechanism to do so. Getting governments, employers and employees alike to understand that local staff wages included the money to pay their tax liabilities and that employees had to pay them was daunting. Helping work out mechanisms to make this happen was even more challenging.

In the former Soviet Union, the employer was omniscient in an employee's life, providing housing, vacation opportunities and other amenities, and "taking care of" employees' pay and taxes. In one masterpiece of creative accounting, one local government representative pressured me to give him my ambassador's social security number, since "the ambassador was the boss and thus responsible for paying employees salaries and their tax liabilities. "Country "X" gets access to the ambassador's salary, deducts taxes for the entire embassy (really how much did he think the ambassador was getting paid?) and all tax matters — resolved. Needless to say, I did not give out the ambassador's social security number.

I held meetings with dozens of embassy employees who raised some pertinent questions: Was the government really going to collect taxes retroactively dating back years? My talking points with the government in that particular country emphasized that: a) this would impoverish its citizens, if they could even get anything out of them; b) this would be extraordinarily complicated; and c) put diplomatically — the citizens hadn't received any benefits for taxes they never paid. In the end, the government agreed to forgive years-old back taxes. The answer to a second question: "Could an employee quit today and not be liable for any back taxes?"

was always no. But the most important question, "How does the system to pay taxes work?" took months to resolve.

In one country, I met frequently with host country officials, over a dozen representatives of other embassies in the country, and a few U.S. Embassy staffers who were willing to try out the new process and report back. One report I shared with all parties was a staffer's creativity in getting a tax ID number *following the local government's guidance.* After months of frustration, she sent her retired father to "sit-in" at one of the offices that was tasked with providing tax ID numbers. The tax office couldn't admit it was not yet ready for prime time, but the retiree wasn't leaving without a tax number for his daughter. He finally came home with a clearly made-up number, a saga that got the government to look at this issue again.

Program rollouts did not, unfortunately, always mesh with capacity and capabilities, resulting in a credibility gap between government announcements and the reality on the ground. I was fortunate to have several great staffers who were willing to work with me and their own government to document discrepancies and work to address them. I was fortunate, too, to be working in countries where the governments appreciated feedback as to how things weren't working and used the information to fix things. No one — from the lowest-paid employee to the highest-ranking government minister — was bullied or blamed for bringing problems to light. This helped identify weaknesses and enabled them to be fixed.

Today in America, I cringe to see the credibility chasm that has opened up between the Trump administration and the American people, and the administration's constant attempts to ignore or bury negative information or to blame others for its shortcomings. At a minimum, the disregard

67

for transparency and honesty in government is testing our democracy and wreaking havoc on its institutions. At the worst, as President Trump contradicts himself and the experts daily, how can we know how best to move forward, including on such critical matters as the 2020 coronavirus pandemic? Lack of strong leadership and clear and consistent guidance explain the United States abysmal record of having one of the highest Covid-19 death rates per capita of any country in the world.

Back in Ukraine, dealing with the inordinate growth of the U.S. embassy could be frustrating. But we worked creatively to overcome obstacles such as buying things with "no new money." We couldn't max out credit cards like private individuals, or borrow money like the federal government. To help outfit and supply this exponentially expanding mission with limited funds, I mixed one part U.S. military drawdown in Europe, several parts persistence and patience, a good sense of humor and a road trip to Germany.

Thanks to the end of the Cold War, the U.S. military in Europe was able to draw down just as U.S. diplomatic missions were growing in the region. The U.S. Regional Support Center (RSC) in Germany was the link that got surplus U.S. military items to needy U.S. diplomatic missions scattered throughout Europe and beyond. Anything that was not nailed down — even including playground equipment — was fair game. So one fine day my maintenance foreman, head auto mechanic and I flew to Germany for a quick supply trip. Our "RSC wish list" included one military surplus vehicle that we were going to load with all our other supplies and equipment, and drive back to Kiev. We had the added bonus of a couple thousand dollars for much-needed items (including car parts, tools, etc.) that we couldn't purchase in Kiev or obtain through the RSC.

A trip to the German equivalent of Home Depot was humorous as my colleagues tried to read the product information for German tools and supplies until I pointed out that — unlike in the former Soviet Union — *everything* was top quality. We filled four shopping carts and jammed the lot into the remaining room in our now-road-ready surplus military vehicle. We set off for Kiev — and promptly got lost for hours. I had been told that Eastern Europe did not have reliable road signs, both for lack of money and to make it just a bit tougher (in those pre-GPS days) for invaders. I now believe this.

A trip home to Ohio that year for some sorely needed rest and relaxation turned into another buying binge. I managed to fill serious holes in our supply and equipment needs at Home Depot, Staples, auto supply and other stores. My sister-in-law was bemused to receive a call from U.S. Embassy Kiev urging her to remind me about toilet seats, and she gamely passed me the message. I happily sent back a dozen American-standard ones, to replace the cheap local ones that frequently broke. I also shipped back dozens of lights and other fixtures for our new embassy apartments, and car parts and other items that we needed to keep post running.

At the end of the day, the hardships and havoc were worth it. Among other things, we supported two official visits by President Bill Clinton, including one where he signed the 1994 US-Russia-Ukraine Trilateral Statement. In this, the United States and Russia agreed to provide security assurances to Ukraine in exchange for Ukraine's commitment to give up its nuclear weapons. Afterwards, I signed off on a $1.2 million check to buy the concrete to fill in missile silos and build housing for demobilized Ukrainian troops. Within two years, almost 2000 nuclear weapons and warheads — 100% — were gone from Ukraine. And yet Russia invaded Ukraine in 2014, defying the 1994 Russia-United States-Ukraine mutual security agreement and damaging U.S. credibility as a reliable partner.

Integrity and credibility are critical to democracy, rule of law, good governance and international agreements, without which peace, prosperity, and security are impossible. In its heyday, the United States had the credibility to bring together nations that promoted peace and prosperity after WWII through the Marshal Plan and the United Nations. U.S. Government credibility stopped a potential nuclear crisis in Cuba and helped end the Cold War. Even as recently as the first Gulf War, the United States brought together an international coalition of 38 countries to stop Saddam's Hussein's rogue regime after it invaded Kuwait. Today, the Trump Administration is seen as an unreliable partner that undermines its allies, voids international treaties, tears down international organizations and alliances and promotes or prolongs wars and conflicts (Afghanistan, Syria, Iran) instead of fostering peace.

Back to that 1994 presidential visit, though, as it truly reflected the craziness that was Kiev.[P9] I set up my command center (my little Toyota Corolla) at the airport, from which I dispatched people and things to deal with crises large and small. For example, I sent my intrepid warehouse manager to snag a blue curtain from an airport snack bar, needed as a back-drop for a presidential photo shoot. Sergey had to assure the manager that President Clinton was *not* going to stop at the snack bar for a burger. Thus, the snack bar manager *could* loan us his blue curtain, and we would make sure he got his curtain back. A January 24, 1994, *Time* magazine article mentioned the snack bar curtain to highlight the challenges of Kiev and our mission, while stressing that we got the job done.[34]

I was sick as a dog that visit, but with a skeleton embassy crew, everyone had to pitch in. When my fever spiked, I stepped out of my car into the frigid Ukrainian winter, and when I started shivering, stepped back into my toasty "command center." I remember ordering pizzas for the visit support teams — and being given rolls of toilet paper, treasured recent newspapers and even official presidential m&ms off of Air Force One in return. We were operating on a shoestring, but it was nice that our work was recognized and appreciated.

In summary, during this tour I helped Ukraine develop basic democratic institutions, supported its development of the rule of law and serious efforts to reduce crime and corruption and helped it get rid of, as noted in that same *Time* magazine article, "175 . . . intercontinental missiles and more than 1,800 nuclear warheads . . . [after] months of painstaking US diplomacy." Given that America has had democracy for 200+ years and is still working to strengthen and improve it, I think the Ukrainians can be quite proud of their progress towards becoming a strong and viable democracy despite continuing challenges that include Russian interference in — and occupation of — their country. In contrast, I was personally mortified to have to explain U.S. government shutdowns over budget issues when I was in Ukraine, not quite the good governance we wanted to model. *Ukrainians* offered to pay our consular officers' salaries during the shutdown so these officers could continue to issue the visas the Ukrainians needed to get to the United States. I had to explain that the U.S. government could not accept foreign monies to pay its staff.

Despite all the hard work, I had fun in Ukraine. I took full advantage of the rich cultural life and other experiences that Ukraine had to offer and particularly enjoyed watercolor lessons with a Ukrainian artist. He provided the lessons, insights into Ukraine and tea, and I provided the chocolate chip cookies. I also travelled to Crimea and other beautiful and historic spots in Ukraine, and even to Moscow and St. Petersburg on a train ride that could have been taken from the classic film, *Dr. Zhivago.*

But on to my next assignments as a more experienced "mid-level" Foreign Service Officer . . . "Back in the USA!"

7

BACK IN THE USA

WASHINGTON, D.C., 1995-1996 AND 1998-2000

I'm taking the liberty of combining two tours in Washington, D.C. into one chapter as I don't need to explain life in America, right? . . . except perhaps to me? After my years overseas, it took me a while to figure out some American commercials and slang had certainly changed. I wasn't as culturally confused, though, as the foreign diplomat who questioned me about all the fresh-air-fiend smokers he noticed in Washington, D.C. I explained the laws against smoking inside federal buildings that sent these smokers outside in sub-zero weather. Lesson reinforced: never assume, and ask if something doesn't quite make sense.

My first Washington assignment was for one year as a Special Assistant to the Assistant Secretary of State for the Bureau of Oceans and International Environmental and Scientific Affairs (OES). The job was as sizable as the title. OES coordinates and implements U.S. foreign policy worldwide in science and technology, and in environmental, health and natural resource protection, including for our oceans and on climate change. Among the wide range of specific global concerns I handled were bio-terrorism; forests, fisheries, food insecurity (famine and near famine), oceans and wildlife conservation; health issues such as avian influenza; science; technology; and the use of outer space. I loved the job and the wonderful people who worked there. This tour was an eye-opening opportunity to make a difference in the world.

A short explanation of Foreign Service bidding is in order to explain my transition from supervising people and managing facilities to dealing with fish, furry critters, oceans and the environment and outer space. While Foreign Service Officers are required to be knowledgeable about a wide range of subjects and to be quick studies, many have areas of deeper expertise. These can be geographic and include language expertise, or they can be "functional" and include expertise on narco-trafficking, visa fraud, international trade negotiation and agreements — or even on setting up new embassies.

The Foreign Service is quite competitive, with an "up-or-out" system in which officers must do well to be promoted or risk losing their jobs. Foreign Servicer Officers must also be available for world-wide service, but they do have some control over their assignments. Towards the end of each tour of duty, they put together a bid list of perhaps 6-10 assignments they would like, ranking them from "most desired" to "ok I'll go there, but not my favorite." Officers bid on those jobs to which they can bring a particular expertise, on jobs in which they know they can excel. Finally, a panel composed of personnel specialists, the appropriate functional representative (consular, political or other officer, or security specialists, etc.), and an officer representing either the post — or the bureau in Washington where the job is located — reviews the applicants, and decides who would be best for the job.

I had a strong background in science from high school and college, and had always been an avid environmentalist. I also was young and single, and thus not too concerned about the long hours the job required. The assignments panel probably looked favorably on my flexibility in handling a number of unexpected temporary assignments in both Mali and Montreal, and figured I should be able to handle the wide range of issues this position covered. I was excited to learn that I'd been accepted for the OES Special Assistant position, one of my top bids.

The second Special Assistant position in OES Bureau was vacant for much of my tour so I generally worked 60-70-hours per week. My workday began early as I skimmed through hundreds of cables, news feeds and other information to reduce them to a pertinent, manageable amount for the OES Bureau's assistant secretary's 8 a.m. arrival. The information I gleaned helped me draft or edit papers on topics ranging from pollution in ocean depths to polar caps, and up to the technological advances supporting our space installations and satellites. Climate change in the 1990s was already a headliner issue that provided me an intense introduction to the press and to other agencies handling the issue. I was grateful daily for my scientific background that helped me understand the issues, keep up with the experts and do a better job.

Working in OES was an advanced class in how government should work. I pushed priority issues, strategized timing and coordinated with other federal agencies, large and small businesses (and everything in between), environmental and other non-governmental organizations, law firms, insurance agencies, the public and other interested parties. In OES, we listened to ensure that their concerns were heard and addressed to the extent possible, while moving forward on U.S. government environmental and scientific goals. No one got everything he or she wanted, but all had a chance to provide input and to impact policy. Senior officials — both Foreign and Civil Service — were often experts in their fields, and carefully crafted policies and explained them so the people we served understood them. The officials I worked with were thoughtful, accountable, and willing to tackle issues including climate change and pollution that had long-term, potentially catastrophic consequences: consequences that we see today, but that weren't as readily apparent then. I also worked closely with congressional offices and the Bureau of Public Diplomacy, which is responsible for advertising and explaining the work of the State Department to international audiences. I gained an appreciation for the importance of both.

The highlight of this assignment was helping host a 1995 United Nations Environment Programme Conference in which representatives from 110 countries *unanimously agreed to take specific measures to protect the world's oceans*.[35] The conference was the culmination of decades of work by thousands of concerned environmentalists and others, but I am proud of my small part in it. For me, this was government at its best. The conference identified the areas most negatively impacted by human activity, focused on a "dirty dozen" of toxic man-made compounds that persisted in the environment (persistent organic pollutants or "POPs"), and came up with specific, viable plans of action to which all participants agreed. More work clearly needs to be done, but this was a major step in the right direction to protect human health, the health of the planet and economic prosperity for the millions of fishermen, tour companies and so many others who depend on the seas and a clean and healthy environment for sustainable living. Oh, and I got to meet avid environmentalist and legendary musician Don Henley of the Eagles!

Office tech continued to be troubling. I was working late one night to get diplomatic notes out to the U.N. conference attendees. Our state-of-the-art-printers couldn't handle the archaic size of diplomatic note paper — slightly longer than regular 8.5x11 letter paper — and kept kicking the paper out before it would print the last two lines. It took two computer techs, one special assistant from another Bureau and me a couple of hours until we figured it out. At that late hour, I knew I'd never get a shorter draft cleared in time to distribute it. So I scrounged an old typewriter from a supply closet, hand-typed the last two lines on each note and sent them out. Thanks to colleagues in the State Department's Legal Bureau, diplomatic notes may now be printed on standard letter-size paper to the relief of thousands of diplomats worldwide. U.S. missions worldwide no longer have to keep stocks of the odd-sized archaic paper, and don't need to keep old typewriters around to type those last few lines from overly long diplomatic notes.

My second Washington assignment, two years in the Office of Sanctions Policy for the Bureau of Economic, Business, and Agricultural Affairs (EB), was also incredible. I was not an economics officer, but I had just returned to the United States after a rover tour serving in over a dozen African countries (next Chapter). The rover tour gave me the invaluable insights to recognize that if we sent night vision goggles to country "X's" police and military forces, they might be used to follow and pick up dissidents leading to human rights violations, and not to "track and capture bad guys" as claimed.

The idea of "dual use technology" was a seminal one for me, and this premise of "duality" still influences my opinions on today's complex issues like nuclear proliferation. Can an item only be used for peaceful nuclear purposes (nuclear medicine or energy, for example), or can it easily be turned into weaponry? If not, go ahead and support its export to the benefit of American industry and the end-user hospital, power plant or other entity. But if a product is too easily turned into deadly weapons, then either re-engineer it — if possible — so it can't be used for harm. Make sure there are guidelines in place to prevent the abuse of an item — or don't license it at all. "Duality" helps me understand today's complicated subjects particularly when I'm faced with so much information that often confuses rather than clarifies an issue.

The skills I'd developed in OES, and those I gained and honed in EB, helped me craft policies to meet key U.S. goals while coordinating with or addressing the concerns of government agencies, business, the public, and other constituencies impacted by these policies. One difference: the sanctions that EB imposed or maintained during my tenure were to counter terrorism, deter military aggression and fight narcotics trafficking and to support human rights, democratization and other key goals. They were generally much higher profile issues, and with shorter-term deadlines that often had much higher costs than the environmental issues I'd dealt with in OES. If we made mistakes in EB, feedback was quick and clamorous. Dealing with Congress, the United Nations and foreign governments, as well as the high-powered lobbyists whose commercial interests were impacted, added to the pressures.

Staffing shortages were also endemic in EB, and added to the stress of this high-pressure environment. I filled a staffing gap for two months to cover India-Pakistan sanctions.

This occurred just as the White House demanded a major revision of a strategic export control list of nuclear, chemical, biological and other weapons of mass destruction in preparation for a presidential visit to India. To quote my annual evaluation for that year, I met "the strict evidentiary and security standards of attorneys and intelligence professionals, made recommendations on programs differentiating between proliferation concerns, dual military/civilian and civilian technologies. Her efforts and decision memoranda drafted for the Deputy Secretary Pickering helped facilitate trade between India and the US, [and] pave the way for a successful Presidential visit to India . . . " Heady stuff for a small-town midwesterner and still relatively new Foreign Service Officer, and it meant long hours of hard work to make sure I got it right.

As in OES, I was privileged to work with some remarkable people, including Under Secretary of State for Economic, Business, and Agricultural Affairs Stuart Eizenstat, as well as Ambassador Alan Larson. Both were amazing practitioners of the art of diplomacy, and I learned so much from them. I first met U/S Eizenstat when several colleagues and I helped prepare him for Congressional testimony. Senior State Department personnel often testify before Congress and elsewhere, and countless hours can go into preparing for these appearances. Congressional testimony can be particularly daunting — and the meetings set up to prepare for such testimony are appropriately called "Murder Boards." My job was to "come up with the questions I thought Congress might ask the U/S about my portfolio — and answer them!" I then attended the session where we put these questions to the Under Secretary and refined the responses. Depending upon the issue, the briefing books could contain dozens of questions and be inches thick.

Fast forward to the day of the testimony, and the U/S's first comments were to — *develop credibility.* He discussed his work in the Carter Administration in 1980, when we "punished" the USSR for its invasion of Afghanistan by not selling it American corn and wheat. He noted that we only hurt America farmers, *not the Soviets*, because Canada, Brazil and other competitors were more than happy to sell their corn and wheat to the Soviet Union — and increase their customer bases by being more reliable suppliers. Congress listened, so he was able to advocate for our proposed sanctions, emphasizing that they were targeted to impact the bad guys and not do inadvertent harm to American business. Further, they had broad international support, and included mechanisms to ensure their effectiveness. In 2020, have we learned anything? Our tariffs against China again directly harm U.S. farmers. Yes, U.S. farmers get compensatory payments now but for how long, and are the payments enough to cover both short-term losses and the incalculable long-term damage to their customer base and their reputation as reliable suppliers?

Personally, I believe in studying history and learning from it, while supporting current best practices and exploiting expertise. For example, I was impressed with Ambassador Larson's use of "virtual" negotiations in the 1990s, when the Internet (which went worldwide in 1991) was still new. He used his expertise and influence with U.S. Embassy Tokyo representatives as well as their Japanese counterparts to ensure that America's concerns and interests were addressed. He took the endless — and expensive — flight to Tokyo only when a final, personal push to conclude negotiations was needed. He coupled his substantive expertise with cutting edge technology to provide real-time guidance in several venues concurrently and saved the U.S.

government tens of thousands of dollars in travel funding alone. He also saved considerable personnel time and wear and tear by not spending endless hours in transit.

A few years later I was stationed in Frankfurt, Germany, where we had weekly video conferences with Washington on a multi-million dollar project to turn a former U.S. military hospital into a major diplomatic facility. Many different players were involved in this project, and we saved tens of thousands of dollars by doing everything virtually that we could. We also saved employees from burnout from constant travel and time zone changes. Teams from Washington did, however, come out as needed.

Prior to the coronavirus pandemic, I was surprised by the number of people who endured lengthy daily commutes or long trips away from family and friends, when the possibilities of the e-world — and its economic and environmental benefits — are so clear. As I write this, the tragic global pandemic may actually influence us all towards a more virtual way of life. Nothing, of course, can replace personal interactions, but a better balance between virtual and physical office presence would be better for people and our planet. Gridlock, pollution, commuting and other costs are reduced and people have more time to spend on family and other more important things.

Some background on ambassadors and their key positions as leaders in the State Department is in order here. Under Secretary Eizenstat was a political appointee, selected by the U.S. president and confirmed in this appointment by the U.S. Senate. Ambassador Larson was a career Foreign Service Officer who had risen through the diplomatic ranks, was selected by the U.S. president, and was then confirmed by the U.S. Senate. Ambassadors have extraordinarily complex and difficult jobs, and not everyone is up to the challenge. They must manage the personnel and resources of the mission; draw upon all the power of the United States (political, military, foreign assistance or other); and utilize their own expertise, power of persuasion and other skills to influence the host country and achieve U.S. foreign policy and national security goals. I remember a joke about an admiral at a reception who told an ambassador that he would like to be an ambassador when he retired from the Navy. The ambassador replied "How interesting, I was hoping to run a battleship in my retirement." Neither job should be taken lightly, or be filled by less than the best.

Today fewer than half of our about 190 senior diplomatic ranks are filled by career professionals. Additionally, the Senate seems to rubber-stamp all appointments, including those of major contributors to political parties, instead of insisting on appointees who actually have the experience and expertise needed to fill these tough jobs. For the health of the State Department and for the strongest American global leadership possible, political appointees should never account for more than one-third of all our senior leadership. Further, the Senate must do a better job vetting ambassadors to ensure that they have the expertise and qualifications relevant to the position. That still provides opportunities for highly qualified outsiders to be ambassadors. In some prestigious posting such as London, Paris and Tokyo, the cost of doing business is so high that being independently wealthy is almost a requirement. The State Department provides basic funding for ambassadors to carry out their duties, but at these high-cost posts this is often not adequate. Wealthy ambassadors, as long as they are *qualified,* can be a benefit to the nation.

Over-use of political assignments, however, harms the State Department at all levels. The State Department is an "up-or-out," hierarchical organization that has many more people at lower levels than at higher ones. To rise to the level of ambassador, an officer must be truly exceptional. When over half the jobs at the top are gone due to political appointments, highly skilled professionals retire or leave for jobs outside the Department. The State Department and the U.S. government are both weakened without their decades of experience and expertise. As China and other countries constantly contest America's power and leadership with their best people and resources, we cannot afford to send less than the best out to lead our missions. Senior U.S. representatives who are not up to the job ruin long-standing relationships, undermine efforts to further U.S. policies, programs and other interests and can do harm that takes years to overcome. The Senate must say "no" to unqualified personnel, no matter how much they may have donated to any political campaign.

Expertise and integrity coupled with good policies and practices make for good diplomacy. I was proud to contribute to National Security Council meetings with staffers from the White House and numerous other U.S. government agencies to develop measures to stop the trade in "blood" diamonds. Blood diamonds were aptly named: they were mined in abusive, appalling conditions and used to fund terrorism and bloody armed conflicts across Africa. I was also proud — albeit initially totally isolated in multi-agency meetings — to be able to influence policy makers not to add sanctions on two countries where existing sanctions were not working. I instead helped persuade them that strengthening and enforcing existing sanctions would both be effective and enhance U.S. credibility, while adding more potentially *ineffective* sanctions would do the reverse. I frequently dealt with Congress too, as when I explained to one Senate staffer why we were denying a constituent a license to sell navigational radios to Sudan. At the time, the Sudanese were allegedly using this technology to bomb civilian targets including hospitals. I worked to get humanitarian supplies to the truly needy and support U.S. business, while denying funding and materials to criminal regimes and supporters of terrorism. Daily, I felt I was having a positive impact.

I also helped complete a comprehensive *computerized* sanctions law table to expedite our office's work. When I began my assignment in the Office of Sanctions Policy, my colleagues and I laboriously researched our customers' requests before we could issue them the licenses they required to sell their products. This was based on the product itself, the country of import and the end-user, with special attention paid if the product could be turned to harmful purposes (the "dual use" issue). We were understaffed, the research took time, and our customers often had lengthy waits for results. By developing the easily searchable computerized table of licensing regulations, the process went more quickly. Today, the Treasury Department's Office of Foreign Assets Control (OFAC) has all this information online so customers can easily determine for themselves if they need licenses to provide their products to a specific buyer — or to look to other customers if licenses clearly could not be issued under existing regulations. Open, transparent government saved the office the time and expense of handling thousands of customer calls annually — and expedited business for customers who no longer had to wait for woefully understaffed offices to get back to them.

One of the most interesting issues I dealt with in the Office of Sactions Policy was one which had implications for the balance of power in America during a presidential election. States rights versus the federal government's Constitutional mandate to conduct foreign policy was the basis of the *Crosby v. National Foreign Trade Council*

(NFTC) lawsuit that went all the way to the Supreme Court in 2000.[36] Massachusetts law prohibited the state from buying goods from any company, domestic *or foreign*, that did business in Burma (Myanmar) in an attempt to isolate its brutal military dictatorship and hopefully, influence it to moderate its behavior. The suit was named for Stephen Crosby, the Massachusetts Secretary of Administration and Finance at the time, while the National Foreign Trade Council is a private organization composed of hundreds of businesses that support free trade among nations.

Congress had already passed a law sanctioning Burma, but Massachusetts, some cities in California and others thought the federal sanctions were too weak against this brutal regime, and so instituted their own. Other states and cities wanted to follow their lead. Officials at the Departments of State and Justice worried that the White House might not support its Constitutional right to conduct foreign policy due to domestic political concerns, including potentially offending California with its critical electoral college votes in the run up to the 2000 presidential election. The optics — that the Democrats were allegedly supporting a brutal regime and money (business) over human rights, and that the federal government was bullying the states — were not good, even though the federal government sanctions against Burma already existed.

In the end the White House filed an amicus brief supporting the premise that the federal government alone — not the states — had the Constitutional authority to sanction a foreign government. The Supreme Court decided unanimously in favor of the NFTC and the Constitution, and Al Gore narrowly lost the 2000 presidential election. I doubt that voters selected their president based on this single issue, but it certainly got public attention.

Interestingly, the attorney for the Commonwealth of Massachusetts compared the Massachusetts law to the Boston Tea Party, colonial America's rebellion against governmental tyranny. He noted that revolutionary action against power for the common good was a time-honored American tradition. The courtroom burst into laughter when Supreme Court Justice Scalia responded that the Supreme Court was a constitutional court, and as the Boston Tea Party occurred well before the constitution was written, that precedent did not apply. Government service was my window on history, often serious and impacting people's lives in ways small and large. But it was never without a humanizing sense of humor.

One digression, if I may. We all know lawyer jokes, but I was impressed with the integrity and work ethics of the attorneys I worked with. I recall one long session working with attorneys on the Supreme Court case. A senior official noticed that we had missed lunch and were fading, and reappeared a short time later with snacks and sodas to keep us going. Lawyers are often blamed for "letting criminals go free" and other injustices. In fact, they are merely enforcing the law. It is *our* duty, through the representatives we elect and our continuing public oversight, to make sure that laws are well-written, properly executed and enforced, and do not enable or permit injustices.

I was also impressed by the Supreme Court justices, and particularly Justice Scalia, who I admired for his decades of service to America and for the fact that, while he was part of America's "elite" his son was serving in the U.S. military. I was honored to be Justice Scalia's control officer when he passed through in Frankfurt, accompanied by his wife and daughter who visited injured troops at Landstuhl Military Hospital.

But — back overseas, and on to Africa.

MEMORIAL WALL
U.S. Department of State, Washington, D.C.

This memorial honors diplomats who died in the service. My good friend Michelle O'Connor was killed in the 1998 bombing of U.S. Embassy in Nairobi, Kenya. 213 other people died and over 4,000 more were injured in this terrorist act.

PLATE 1

My Junior Officer class after we took our oath of office, Diplomatic Reception Rooms, U.S. Department of State, Washington, D.C. I am at the far right.

PLATE 2

PLATE 3

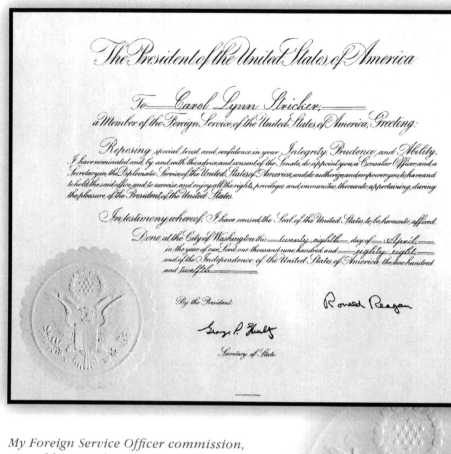

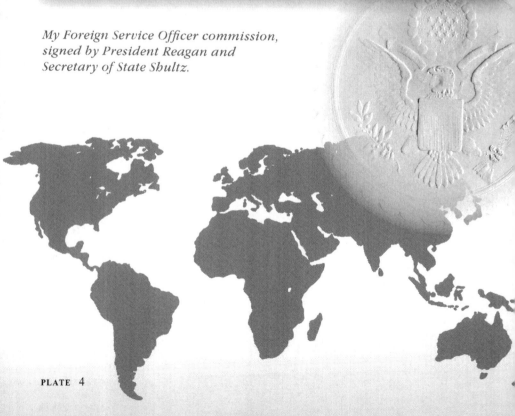

My Foreign Service Officer commission,
signed by President Reagan and
Secretary of State Shultz.

PLATE 4

Getting to work (or play) could be a challenge, Bamako, Mali.

Checking up on a water reservoir/ agricultural project, northern Mali.

Crisis management exercise, Lagos Nigeria. This exercise prepared embassy personnel for all aspects of crises, including, "how to get out of town if needed!"

PLATE 5

UNESCO World
Heritage site
Djenne mosque.

PLATE 6

The docks at Segou.

Riverboat trip, Niger river, Mali. The entire town turns out to meet our boat.

PLATE 7

Road trip, "road" not necessarily included.

Other modes of transportation, from canoe and ferry to U.S. military attaché plane.

PLATE 8

U.S. President Bill Clinton's January 1994 official visit to Kiev, Ukraine.

Embassy staff with me in my bright blue beret.

PLATE 9

The crane
that fell on
my office
trailer.

U.S. Embassy Kiev, a construction site inside and out,
which made for interesting working conditions.

PLATE 10

River rafting on the Zambezi river, Zambia

*"Suited up"
for swimming
with dolphins,
Mozambique.*

*UNESCO World Heritage sites Samarkand
and Bukhara, Uzbekistan on the old Silk
Road to China.*

*Raptor rescue
center, Uzbekistan*

PLATE 11

Ancient "Supercroc' fossil, discovered by Dr. Paul Sereno of the University of Chicago, northern Niger.

Medieval meets modern times, northern Niger Tuareg festival.

The Dabous giraffe, one of hundreds of amazing ancient rock carvings.

Time for tea.

PLATE 12

U.S President George W. Bush's May 2005 visit to Tbilisi Georgia, with Georgian President Mikheil Saakachvili at Freedom Square.

Sensational Georgian dancers.

Photos courtesy of Professor Ed McLuskie.

PLATE 13

Meeting and greeting, public speaking . . .

FOREIGN SERVI
INSTITUTE

United States
Department of State

The Secretary's Career Achievement Award
is presented to

Carol L. Stricker

In recognition of her twenty-five years of distinguished service to the
U.S. Department of State and the Foreign Service.

November 2010

Hillary Rodham Clinton
Secretary of State

...are just a few of
the many duties of
a diplomat's job.

PLATE 14

CAR PARK

UGANDA

STATE VISIT BY
E UNITED STATES PRESIDENT
TO UGANDA

SECRETARY
OFFICE OF THE PRESIDENT

PLEASE BRING THIS CARD WITH YOU

THE REPUBLIC OF UGANDA

550

The President of The Republic of Uganda,
H. E. Yoweri Kaguta Museveni
requests the pleasure of the company of

graced by the presence of the Visiting President of The United States of America,
William Jefferson Clinton and Mrs. Hillary Rodham Clinton

Date: 24th March, 1998
Venue: Kisowera Primary Sch...

ЧУМХУРИИ
ТОҶИКИСТОН

VISA № 0256

To ду мох / Till tw...

STRICKER CARO...
Рақами шиносома / Passport No 90...
Навъ / Type ДИПЛОМАТ
Вуруд - Entry - Хуруҷ / Exit - Вуруд / Ent...
Таърихи судур / Date of issue
01.10.2003   01.12.2003

Хампох / Accompanied by

U.S.
EMBASSY
ACCRA

Carol STRICKER
NAME
ADMIN/STATE
SECTION

№: 0161
Frank DeMichele
RSO

GRATUIT

AMBASSADE
REPUBLIQUE DU NIGER
WASHINGTON, D.C.

ISA: 504
PRENOM: STRICKER CAROL
DU VISA: DIPLOMATIQUE
POUR SEJOUR: DOUBLE/MULTIPLE
3 MOIS   EM
IQUE DU NIGER A COMPTER
D'ENTREE 13 Août 2000
SUR PRESENTATION DANS LES
ENT LA DATE

EMBASSY
OF THE
UNITED STATES OF AMERICA
Kinshasa, Zaire

STRICKER, CAROL L.

C OF UZBEKIST...

№ 213746
D-2
.10.2003   DAN
UNTIL 30.09.200...
SONI
OF ENTRIES Multiple
AT MUDDATI 90
N OF STAY   KUN
DAYS
N JOYI Berlin TARIXI 25.09...
RAQAMI 900374332 ON
RT No.

American Embassy
Maputo, Mozambique

CAROL...

31 DECEM...

C. Stricker

VISA DIPL...

Entries/Entrés   Departures/Sorties

Visas

AMBASSADE DU MALI
Washington - U.S.A.

ture Visa: Diplomatique
Visaa ○26/AMW/88
te: 31 MAR 1988
able ol semaine á compter
la date d'arrivée pour une
ule entrée

2 AVR 19
MALI

Министерство закордонних с...
України
УПРАВЛІННЯ ДЕРЖАВН...
ПРОТОКОЛУ
ДИПЛОМАТИЧНА КА...
№ 1-1123/9...

საქართველოს საგარეო საქმეთა სამინისტროს
დიპლომატიური პროტოკოლის დეპარტამენტი
Ministry of Foreign Affairs of Georgia
Diplomatic Protocol Department
DIPLOMATIC CARD
№ 1422

Validity. 25.10.2006
DIRECTOR OF DEPARTMENT

Entries/Entrés   Departures/Sorties

Visas

CONSULADO DA REPUBLICA
DE ANGOLA EM Washington DC

VISTO DIPLOMATICO 479/2498

VALIDO PARA 2(Duas) ENTRADA(S)
E UM TOTAL DE PERMANENCIA DE 30 (TRINTA)
DIAS

UTILIZAVEL NO PRAZO DE 60
DIAS, A CONTAR DA DATA DA SUA
CONCESSAO SOB PENA DE CADUCIDADE

CONSULADO DA REPUBLICA DE ANGOLA
Washington 09 de OUTUBRO de 1996
EMBAIXADOR

3479

INTERNATIONAL CERTIFICATE OF VALI...
AGAINST YELLOW...
CERTIFICAT INTERNATIONAL DE VA...
CONTRE LA FIÈV...

tify that
certifie que

re follows
ure suit

indicated been vaccinated or revaccinated against yellow...
ou revaccine(e) contre la fièvre jaune à la date indiquée.

Signature and professional status
of vaccinator
Signature et titre du
vaccinateur

1987   Eben H. Dustin...
Med. Division Dept. of State
Washington, D.C.

VACCINATION CENTER
No. 18
U.S.A.

From an invitation from Ugandan
President Yoweri Museveni to a
reception for U.S. President Bill
Clinton, through embassy I.D.s and
visas to my international certificate
of vaccinations, no bureaucracy is
complete without its paperwork.

ДВ № 0019265

ПАСПОРТТЫҢ №/PASSPORT №
900374331

ӘЗIМЕН БIРГЕ/ACCOMPANIED BY

ZATIONS/PROPHYLAXIS RECEIVED
ation/prophylaxies reçues

obulin, malaria, measles, etc.)

Vaccine/prophylactic
drug
Vaccin/drogue prophylactique

Signature du médecin

ШАҚЫРҒАН МЕКЕМЕ/INVITING ORGANIZATION

БЕРIЛГЕН КҮНI/DATE OF ISSUE
06

ҚОЛЫ мен ТЕГІ/SIGNATURE and SURNAME

1987	ТОРУ Ⓑ	2cc.	Eben H. Dustin, M.D.
1987	typhoid Ⓑ	0.1cc	Eben W. Dustin, MD
1987	Gamma Glob.	1.5	Eben H. Dustin, MD
1987	1st dip	0.5	Eben H. Dustin M.D.
1988	gamma glob.	5cc	Eben W. Dustin, MD

YPE
КІРУ
entry
multiple

ECI/ENTRIES

СТАЛУ МЕРЗІМІ/VALID FROM 2003
СТАЛУ МЕРЗІМІ/VALID UNTIL 2004

СЫМША МӘЛІМЕТТЕР/ADDITIONAL INFORMATION

PLATE 13

Treasures

From my Ukrainian staff, a "Mother hero of the Soviet Union Award" given to mothers with large families in the former Soviet Union. The bronze plaque reads "with love to Mama GSO, Kiev, Ukraine, June 1995.

THE WHITE HOUSE
WASHINGTON

June 14, 1995

Ms. Carol Stricker
Embassy of the United States of America
Yuri Kotsubinskiy St., 10
254353, Kiev
UKRAINE

Dear Carol:

Thank you for your help during my trip to Kiev.

I know how much time and energy it takes to coordinate a Presidential visit, and I appreciate all of your efforts to ensure that this one went smoothly.

I'm grateful for your support and send my best wishes.

Sincerely,

Bill Clinton

Thank you note from President Bill Clinton from his official 1994 visit to Kiev, Ukraine.

From my Malian staff, a toolkit complete with canoe (lower left), ladder (far right), mortar and pestle, knife (blade retracted), and the essential good luck charm (center).

PLATE 16

8

UKRAINE AND AFRICA:
COMPARE AND CONTRAST
A TIMELESS OVERVIEW

My next assignment was a two-year roving tour for the State Department's Bureau of African Affairs. In stays of anywhere from a couple of weeks to a couple of months, I covered as many as three to four jobs simultaneously in ten countries across Africa to try and fill gaping holes in staffing at U.S. diplomatic missions. Setting up 13 new missions in the former Soviet Union with no new staffing or added funding had worldwide implications, as personnel and money were taken from established posts to set up the new ones. The negative impact was particularly severe on U.S. missions in Africa. To help embassies maintain operations and move forward on U.S. goals, the Bureau of African Affairs had three "roving" officers, jacks-or-jills!-of-all-trades with the proven ability and willingness to tackle any challenges.

But first, dear reader, to help you better understand this crazy, chaotic tour, I'd like to provide you a bit of background information on a continent that is relatively unknown to many Americans — myself included prior to my work there. The following are some insights into Africa, beginning with some interesting parallels I found between Ukraine and the many African countries in which I served.

To begin, I give you centuries of Ukrainian history in a nutshell.[37] The Museum of Historical Treasures of Ukraine in Kiev holds an impressive collection of Scythian gold jewelry that could match anything Fabergé created in beauty, artistry and craftsmanship. The jewelry and other artifacts date from the eighth century BCE to the second century CE. In the ninth century CE, the Kievan Rus federation introduced Christianity to its people and grew to be one of the largest empires in Europe. Then came the Mongols (think Gengis Khan), who sacked and pillaged the rich city of Kiev, killing most of its population in 1240. After the Mongols, the Grand Duchy of Lithuania, Kingdom of Poland and Ottoman Empire ruled parts of Ukraine until the Russian Empire annexed it in 1783. The Soviets ruled Ukraine from 1922 until 1991, with a nadir in 1932-33 when millions of Ukrainians died of starvation under forced collectivization. In WWII, millions of Ukrainians, including most of its Jewish population, were killed and Kiev was again destroyed. So: glory days followed by invasion, occupation and pillaging, and yet Ukraine's indomitable people continue to survive and even prosper.

Indomitable people who experienced exceptional highs and terrible lows of history were something I saw again in Africa. Examples of growth followed by invasion exist across the Continent. Timbuktu and Djenne were rich centers of trade, religion and learning in a Malian Empire that lasted for hundreds of years (1235-1670). The Empire of Ghana lasted from 300-1100. Their artistry and craftsmanship are reflected in the gold jewelry worn even today and featured in the book *Africa Adorned* that I so admired. In two darker decades (1885-1905) of colonial occupation and exploitation, King Leopold of Belgian plundered the Congo's natural riches for his own ends and his policies led to the deaths of millions of Congolese. The Zulu Empire (1816-1897) in what today is South Africa was brought down by the British. Zulus and many others later suffered under South Africa's apartheid regime, and today are still trying to overcome its terrible legacies.

In other parallels, all the trials and tribulations of my tours in the former Soviet Union — lack of infrastructure, little support and funding for basic services, and threats from terrorism, disease and natural disasters — were also reflected in Africa. And yet I couldn't have chosen a better time to be a diplomat. In Germany, the Berlin Wall fell, and former Soviet satellites relished their newfound freedom. They shared a sense of optimism as they looked to the United States and the West for models of democracy and good governance that would serve as their foundations for prosperity and peace. In Africa, I saw this optimism in many countries as they, too, moved towards democracy, good governance and economic prosperity. In both regions, I was welcomed as an American, with America's government and economic prosperity admired and emulated. Both were worth more than any propaganda.

There were, of course, undeniable contrasts. Africa contains many countries with significantly different histories, cultures, geography, political systems, and both natural and political barriers to progress. For example, even in the 1990s, flights between former French colonies in western Africa and former British colonies in eastern Africa where rare. To get from francophone Mali to anglophone Malawi

(5,000 miles), for example, you would have to fly 3,800 miles (mostly north) to Paris and then a further 7000 miles (south and east) to Lilongwe. In other words, you had to fly double the distance, with an inconveniently long layover in Paris, to go from former French to former British colonial Africa. Add in tribalism, weak institutions (government, education, healthcare), poor infrastructure, poor and often corrupt leadership, disease (HIV AIDS, Ebola, malaria, etc.), drought and other disasters, and terrorism — the obstacles Africans needed to overcome were, and continue to be, daunting.

Slavery, both from the colonial legacy and among Africans themselves, left an indelible mark on Africa. U.S. embassies never discriminate in hiring, so we hired dark-skinned Africans for professional positions in one country where darker-skinned citizens were generally limited to manual labor and other less prestigious jobs. The Embassy benefitted from these capable employees, but their own country was poorer for not valuing them. In another country, one embassy employee pointed out a colleague and said, "My father used to own his father." And in yet a third country, two people were selected for host country civil service positions after an "unbiased" exam was held. I was told by two local national embassy employees who studied diligently for this exam that the two people who were selected for the positions didn't even bother to show up and take it. Africans will need the strength, resilience and the capabilities of all its people to progress on their path towards good governance and prosperity.

United Nations Secretary General Kofi Annan, the first African to hold this position, perfectly reflected my thinking on Africa in his speech before an Organization of African Unity Summit in June, 1997.[38] He talked, for example, of the "three waves" of African history and of what it will take for African nations to succeed.

> First came decolonization and the struggle against apartheid. Then came a second wave, too often marked by civil wars, the tyranny of military rule, and economic stagnation. I believe that a new era is now in prospect, Africa's third wave. Let us make this third wave one of lasting peace, based on democracy, human rights, and sustainable development.

I felt that I was part of the third way, and I saw positive change in many African countries, including on human rights. Again, the Secretary General captured my thoughts in his speech:

> I am aware of the fact that some view this [human rights] concern as a luxury of the rich countries for which Africa is not ready. I know that others treat it as an imposition, if not a plot, by the industrialized West. I find these thoughts truly demeaning, demeaning of the yearning for human dignity that resides in every African heart. Do not African mothers weep when their sons or daughters are killed or maimed by agents of repressive rule? Are not African fathers saddened when their children are unjustly jailed or tortured? Is not Africa as a whole impoverished when even one of its brilliant voices is silenced? We cannot afford to lose one life, spare one idea, relinquish one hope, if we are to succeed on our chosen course.

He insists that democracy and good governance, including rule of law and respect for human rights, are essential to any nation, and he highlights the importance of education, healthcare, security and the sustainable use of countries' resources to economic growth and prosperity. Hmmm . . . sounds pretty much like the State Department's mission statement to "create a more secure, democratic and prosperous world" — doesn't it?

So why am I optimistic on Africa? I will provide specific examples in the following chapters, but to continue with this general overview, I saw progress in numerous countries in five key areas. The first and most important was the rise of more democratic and accountable governments, and a decrease in corruption and abuse of power by privileged elites. In Ghana, I served as an election observer along with hundreds of Ghanaians to ensure the integrity of their 1996 presidential election. One observer was a Ghanaian journalist who had been jailed and abused by a previous regime. In the Democratic Republic of the Congo, staff rushed to let me know that the new president's daughters were at the Consulate applying for visas — and were *waiting in line* instead of jumping the line accompanied by gun-toting guards as would have happened under the previous regime. That sent a powerful message that the elite would not bully their way into special treatment and privilege.

Secondly, adopting and implementing better economic policies helped. Certainly, some countries continued to have bad policies and corrupt regimes that were enriching themselves to the detriment of their citizens. But I saw African countries working with the United States, the World Bank, the International Monetary Fund (IMF) and other international partners to fight corruption, make and implement laws to protect small land- and business-owners, and to develop and strengthen banks. Banks would no longer fund dictatorial binge buying.

In several countries, I shopped at small cooperatives

that were begun — and later taken internationally on the Internet — by U.S. Peace Corps volunteers. Micro-lending programs were empowering women via support for their small businesses. And at the individual level, families in richer African countries were becoming smaller. As parents explained to me, they could feed, educate and pay for health care for one or two children, who would then likely survive to take care of the parents in their old age. This was quite different from poorer countries where large families could only hope a few children out of many might survive to take care of their parents. Interestingly, this idea, and model "new way" seemed to spread by word of mouth, and not through any official "smaller families make sense" program. As the prosperity and good governance of the United States spoke for itself, so too did the example of a few healthy and well-educated children surviving childhood to prosper.

Thirdly, the outside influence from the World Bank and other institutions moved from a heavy-handed, dogmatic approach to more collaborative agreements that focused on reducing and mitigating poverty. Better agreements and policies led to growth which helped decrease debt in a continuously positive cycle. Positive growth made the countries attractive to developmental and other organizations and international businesses, which led to even more growth.

A fourth key element was the rise of the Internet and other technologies that were a game changer in Africa. In many of the countries in which I served, cellphones were everywhere. Many entrepreneurs couldn't afford the old-style brick and mortar store-fronts, but they could operate successful businesses from their cellphones. Everyone from entrepreneurs to farmers could take orders, fill them in a timely manner, and coordinate with their suppliers and customers in a seamless chain.

And finally, the youth of the country and the new generation of activists, in politics, business, the arts, media and local communities were an inspiration. They were smart, educated (school attendance and literacy rates were up in many countries in which I served), high-energy and creative, and had a global view that showed them both possibilities and how to accomplish them.

Two steps forward then, and one step back. HIV/AIDs took a tremendous toll on many African countries in which I served. But countries fought back, and we were proud to partner with them in their struggle. I gave one speech in French on HIV/AIDs on national television, as part of a local government program which highlighted the measures people could take to protect themselves and help stop this epidemic. I admired many people in the U.S. Agency for International Development (USAID) who were on the front lines in this and other healthcare battles. HIV/AIDS, malaria and other seemingly intractable diseases, although not eradicated, were successfully controlled. Progress on this front, however, continued to be offset by the rise of new diseases and other health threats.

I am, thus, optimistic about Africa, but am also a realist who fully recognizes that major hurdles remain before Africa can enjoy full peace and prosperity. The rise of terrorism is of particular concern to Africa, as it feeds on the young and the hopeless. I have seen that diplomacy can bring opportunity and hope to countries, and believe that diplomacy working to ensure peace and prosperity is crucial and cost effective in fighting terrorism. From the bombings of the U.S. embassies in Nairobi, Kenya, and Dar es Salaam, Tanzania, to attacks on hotels, businesses, military, police, aid workers and even on farmers in their fields, terrorism creates insecurity that impacts the governmental, security, economic, civic and other institutions that form the foundation of a strong democracy. Terrorism provides little promise of a better future, and historically terrorists who attained power did not build but destroyed, bringing hardship and suffering to the people under their control. Diplomacy can help counter the evils and destruction of terrorism.

I flew out of Nairobi at the end of my rover tour, on August 7, 1998. Ten hours later, more than 200 people were killed and hundreds more injured in the bombings of the U.S. embassies in Nairobi, Kenya, and Dar es Salaam, Tanzania. My good friend Michelle Deney O'Connor was killed in the attack, and had my schedule been slightly different, I might have been with her. In 2000, terrorists killed Bill Bultemeier, a friend who was working with me at the U.S. Embassy in Niger. This book is dedicated to them, and I will never forget their goodwill, good humor, love of life and exemplary service to their country. I will never forget the many people I knew across Africa who were also targeted by, and are fighting against, these same terrorists. The United States has lost opportunities to join in with Africans, Muslims and others who are as dedicated to fighting this terrorism as we are.

Security was a concern throughout my career, and lessons learned from my earlier years as a State Department counterterrorism intelligence analyst helped me stay safe. One essential lesson was to "be unpredictable" in my daily routines. A terrorist debrief I'd read explained why the terrorist had targeted a military officer instead of what might have been considered an "easier" civilian target. He said the civilian was "too alert and unpredictable" to target, while the methodical military officer was not. The "soft" target was constantly varying his timing (he had the chaos of getting his kids ready for school each morning), his routing (he always had stops to make on the way to or from the office), and was constantly checking his car (for car bombs, thought the terrorist). When asked, the "soft target" was able to explain that he did check around his car each morning so he wouldn't run over any of his children's toys.

What is different and scarier today is that diplomats — and medical professionals, fire fighters, the police and other first responders — are no longer the protected people, but have become primary targets of terrorists. I first learned of this frightening aspect of terrorism as a counterterrorism security analyst reading about the delayed bombings that were occurring in the Middle East. Terrorists would commit a suicide strike or car bombing, and then detonate a second bomb, harming the first responders who were trying to help the victims of the first strike.

Freedom and democracy, good government and rule of law, transparency and equal opportunity for all is, for me, our best defense — and offense — against the scourge that is terrorism. Giving people hope and the opportunity for prosperity and a better life can turn them away from terrorism, and towards building and maintaining a more peaceful and prosperous world. And I — along with so many of my colleagues — was willing to work long hours under tough conditions to stop terrorism and keep the United State safe. I wanted my friends, family and all Americans to be safe; *not* to have to think of things like getting blown up or shot while getting ready to go to work, going to the grocery store, or while flying home for the holidays . . .

One final comparison, as I bring this overview on Africa to a close. In the United States we have had many advantages, yet we too are still working to perfect our own democracy. It took us almost a century to end slavery, women and minorities are still fighting for justice and equal rights and we all must exercise constant vigilance against corruption and to maintain and strengthen our democratic institutions. Africa still has a long, hard journey ahead, but I was honored to work with Africans, and proud of what we accomplished together during what was a demanding but exciting period.

So, dear readers, with this as background, please join me on my next assignment, a roving tour across the fascinating continent that is Africa.

9

THE EVEN WILDER WEST —
AND EAST, SOUTH AND CENTRAL
AFRICA, 1996-1998

As noted previously, my "rover" tour was to try and cover huge staffing gaps at U.S. missions across Africa. I had extended stays at ten different countries during this two-year tour, and return visits to several of them. I thought of my service as a "roving trouble-shooter" for the Bureau of African Affairs, and troubles were legion. I did my best, however, to mitigate the harm the staffing gaps and lack of funding caused to U.S. global interests and to further U.S. goals in Africa.

A description of a rover from my annual employee evaluation perfectly captured the essence of the job:

> Given the differing sizes, staffing patterns, geographic locations, political climates, language and local infrastructure, every post in Africa has its own peculiar needs and its unique operating pattern. The rover must be able to adapt instantly . . . with little or no overlap

with the regularly assigned officer . . . the rover must be administrative officer, general services officer, personnel officer, building services specialist . . . and security officer . . . they must be unusually efficient, self-reliant and adaptable — not just once in a while, but every day.

Sounds crazy, right? Please note that I did careful research into the job before applying for it. I had, however, talked to former rovers who filled this position before the State Department increased its staffing gaps exponentially by opening 13 new posts in the former Soviet Union with no money or new staff. When I was bidding on my next assignment as my time as a Special Assistant in the Bureau of Oceans and International Environmental and Scientific Affairs drew to a close, I jumped at the chance to enjoy what sounded like a challenging — but doable — tour across Africa.

Think back to my previous overview of bidding on Foreign Service assignments. My success in concurrently covering a number of different jobs in Mali and Montreal, my work as Special Assistant in Washington, D.C., and the work I'd done in Kiev must have made them think I'd be able to handle this job. The fact that I had good French for an assignment to a continent where many people spoke French, probably helped.

My success in this demanding tour was also helped considerably by my remarkable boss, supporting me from her Bureau of African Affairs office back in Washington, D.C. Her extraordinary knowledge of Africa and logistical wizardry ensured that I was always in the right place at the right time to keep U.S. missions going on a shoestring — and she always made sure I had the shoestring. She was always in the office by 7 a.m. to accommodate an up-to-6-hour-time difference with her rovers, and was always able to help me with my urgent questions and concerns. I particularly appreciated her skill in forwarding my mail to me at each post, given that letters could take a least a month to get to me. And I loved her candor. Her response when I protested her pulling me out of one post which still had issues: "Don't worry," she said "You're really needed in country 'X' where it's much worse" . . . and she was right.

During my two roving years, I filled up to three positions concurrently at several posts, and at one memorable post, I served in four positions at the same time. These assignments were determined purely by the priority needs of the State Department. For editorial convenience, I will share my adventures with you alphabetically. If you get whiplash, my apologies. By the end of the tour I felt a bit like a yo-yo myself.

Embassy **Accra in Ghana** was so short-staffed that officers feared there wouldn't be anyone available to write their annual evaluations. This could have hurt their careers, so I lobbied Washington to get approval to write their evaluations myself. The officers provided me lists of their main accomplishments which I confirmed independently, and the ambassador reviewed and signed off on the final evaluations.

If you'll recall from Chapter Two, diplomats aren't hired for who they know, but for *what* they know, and how effective they can be. Diplomacy can be defined as *the application of power and use of skills to achieve US foreign and national security goals.* Knowledge is part of that power, and knowledge and the skills to apply it are first tested in the rigorous exam that applicants must pass to become diplomats. Then, diplomats undergo an annual review to ensure that they still have the knowledge and skills needed to do the job, that they are using them successfully, and, in this "up-or-out" service, that they have shown their potential to excel at even more senior levels. The officers in Ghana were doing superior work covering numerous and lengthy staffing gaps, including at higher grade levels, and they deserved recognition for their hard work.

A quick note on the exam and the annual evaluation process is in order here. Both measure an extensive depth and breadth of knowledge and expertise. More importantly, both also measure the potential to succeed, and I have rarely met a diplomat who was not able rise to any occasion and handle any contingency.

The Foreign Service Exam is rigorous and comprehensive, covering job-specific expertise such as politics, economics, management principles, world history, current events and geography. It tests for everything a diplomat must know to professionally represent the United States and advocate for it, including U.S. history, politics, government, and culture. English composition and grammar are assessed to ensure that applicants have that core element of successful diplomacy — the ability to communicate well. Beyond that, interpersonal skills, the ability to negotiate, situational awareness and good judgement are evaluated in an intensive role-playing exercise and personal interview. According to the American Foreign Service Association (AFSA), in recent years about 17,000 applicants have taken the test annually, and only 1,000 are invited back for the oral exam. Fewer than that then pass medical and security reviews and are actually offered jobs.[39]

Once diplomats are hired, they are evaluated annually by an independent panel made up of their peers plus one member from outside the Foreign Service. This exercise reviews the diplomat's current performance and his or her continuing professional development and demonstrated ability to take on added responsibilities and operate at higher levels. Diplomats who do not demonstrate this can be recommended for separation. The world is constantly changing, and the professional diplomat must change with it. He or she must be able to use new technologies to better reach host country audiences and influencers, to discern new trends and issues, and to identify potential problems or unexpected opportunities to be able to address them. The attributes that the State Department looks for in its new hires, and that it reviews annually, are attributes that helped me succeed in this demanding rover — and other — tours. Being conscientious, curious about foreign cultures and people and working hard are also essential to diplomacy.

For my colleagues, then, writing their evaluations at U.S. Embassy Ghana was critical. I also kept busy with "normal" management activities to keep the embassy running, and was honored to serve as an election observer for the Ghanaian 1996 presidential elections. The Ghanaian journalist who'd been jailed under an earlier regime and other Ghanaian observers were determined that these elections would be free and fair. Designated observers from each political party as well as international observers were welcomed at each polling station, and I was impressed by Ghanaian professionalism. In one instance, four feet were clearly seen below a voting booth. The election officials quickly figured out that a poor elderly couple was sharing their only pair of glasses, and all observers concurred that no fraud was involved. More critically, poll officials swung into action to ensure polling stations that were running out of ballots due to high turn-out got the ballots they needed. Finally, polling officials also managed to quickly obtain the official authorization needed to stay open with proper oversight until the last voters at these overwhelmed polling stations had voted.

I was dismayed when I returned home some months

later to hear about my sister's electoral experience in the United States. First, she was almost not able to vote as she shared a first — but *not* middle — name and address with my mother. That issue was finally resolved, but she got home just in time to hear reports of polling stations that had run out of ballots before they'd run out of voters. In 2020 and beyond, we must do better.

I can't repeat often enough that freedom is not free. It requires funding and tending. The people, places and mechanisms necessary for voting, a linchpin of American democracy, need to be maintained and secured. Unjustified disenfranchisement, gerrymandering, aging and faulty election infrastructure and other issues that undermine the integrity of vote must be addressed.

My next stop was at Embassy **Bujumbura, Burundi**. I had to take a UN flight in because you couldn't get there from . . . anywhere! A 1996 coup overthrew president Sylvestre Ntibantunganya, and international sanctions prevented law-abiding airlines from landing there. When I was working sanctions policy back in Washington D.C., though, I would remember that airport as one where many *disreputable* airlines flew in with goods to take advantage of skyrocketing prices in this isolated country. When I had the guests over for dinner one night, they brought me a much-appreciated $3 Snickers bar.

As I mentioned in the last chapter, I had to fly from East Africa to West — and vice versa — usually via Paris. It seemed as if my assignments always required me to take long trips with stop-overs to fly across Africa, instead of letting me take short, direct flights to nearby countries. Air travel and lengthy waits in airports provided many colorful moments. In one country, the African gentleman next to me in the waiting area loudly voiced his concerns about our female pilot — and his hands started to shake when he realized the copilot was a woman also. He was quite relieved when we landed successfully, and I hope that flight provided him food for thought about female professionalism. In one interesting Air France flight, a French ambassador on board was complaining that France's iconic air carrier had been "taken over by the Spanish." Air France had subcontracted the flight and the entire crew spoke Spanish — although they could handle French quite well too.

Also memorable was a crowded, chaotic flight serving pilgrims returning from a trip to Mecca. Hours of delay extended what would have been an 8-hour trip to fifteen hours, and we had to deal with a cabin crowded with pilgrims, their huge bags of souvenirs and — I swear — several live animals. Additionally, we had an elderly gentleman who insisted on praying at the top of his voice at 2:00 a.m. A younger gentleman finally spoke gently with him (I was traveling with an Arabic speaker who translated the conversation), noting that Allah both would hear him if he prayed more quietly, and would probably appreciate the respect thus shown to his fellow passengers who were trying to sleep.

In one worst-case scenario we didn't even get off the ground. I, along with several other members of the embassy including the ambassador, got on a plane for a midnight departure. Eight sweltering hours later, the airline admitted that they weren't able to fly out and finally let us off the plane. By that time, unfortunately, even the ambassador's driver had left the airport — which was totally against the rules — and we waited another hour or so for embassy drivers to return to the airport to pick us up.

Two scary scenarios fortunately ended well. In one dangerous post, no one showed up at the airport — for hours

— to pick me up. Fortunately, airport security and the airplane crew were aware of my dilemma and introduced me to someone's "uncle" who could take me to the Embassy. So I got into what barely counted as a vehicle (most of the floor, among other things, was missing), and we putt-putted off to the embassy in the middle of the night. Someone, somehow must have gotten through to the embassy, though, because after a half hour on the road, I saw a powerful embassy vehicle bearing down on us and I urged the driver to start flashing his lights. The embassy vehicle flew by us, braked, reversed course and in the end gave me a ride to my temporary housing, after I'd given the "uncle" a substantial tip.

It turns out that one of my roving colleagues had taken a week off to climb Mt. Kilimanjaro and hadn't checked his cable traffic at the embassy after his vacation. He thus missed the cable that *changed his assignment* at the last minute. So my roving colleague showed up for what was now my assignment. The embassy picked him up at the airport, settled him in temporary housing, and thought they were done for the day. The goods news in all this is that my roving colleague and I got to exchange colorful stories before he left the next day for his revised assignment.

In the second scary incident from a later assignment, I was on a plane that — after one loud bang and a serious shudder — began to lose altitude. The pilot managed to level the plane and make an unscheduled landing at a small airfield in Outer Mongolia. Dozens of armed soldiers watched us as we watched them while the plane was fixed. We left a few hours later, to the relief of everyone involved. I would note that everything is relative. This was a *good* flight as we did not crash.

On another flight when I was (mentally) whining about the three days of leave I would need just to travel home for vacation and then back to post, I was seated next to a U.S. soldier also returning to the United States on vacation. It was going to take him almost a week to do his round trip, he'd been in both Iraq and Afghanistan, and he'd been pulled out on assignments so rapidly he hadn't been able to attend his own wedding nor had he met his newborn son. I stopped my mental whining and gave thanks for my much less demanding career.

But - back to **Burund**i and **Bujumbura's** airport, where I was met by an American military officer. He took me to my temporary housing, from which I was to drive him back to the airport so he could leave post. No worries, I thought. I got this. I drove him back to the airport, returned to my temporary housing without getting lost and made it an early night so I'd be ready for work in the morning.

I arrived at the embassy's Administrative Annex the next morning around 7:00 a.m, carrying my heavy, lunch-box-sized emergency radio. I left it in my office, as it was a bit much to carry as I scouted out the Annex. I made some important discoveries, including the location of the "executive washroom," and that there were NO keys to any of my vehicles in case we needed to evacuate the mission. With raging inflation in Burundi, vehicles, fuel and anything that wasn't nailed down were prime targets for theft, so the motor pool supervisor had been taking the keys home with him to prevent this. This was not as wise as it seemed.

Shortly after 8:00 a.m. I had to call the embassy security post to ask: "What does it mean when no one shows up for work?" The guard told me that they'd been trying to reach me on my emergency radio (carefully stashed in the office where I couldn't hear it). They had not expected me to get to the office an hour early to orient myself on that first day, and had been trying to alert me to the landmines that had been planted in potholes on the roads I'd just traveled over to get to the Annex. All Embassy personnel (except me!) had been told not to report to work until after 10 a.m., by which time the landmines would have been cleared. If the security situation worsened and we had needed to evacuate, all the keys for the embassy vehicles were on the opposite side of town, on the wrong side of the land-mine-strewn main road. No worries, I thought: we could always hot wire the cars and break in to the fuel tank to fuel the cars and get out of town. Interestingly, my class T-shirt from my Foreign Service Officer orientation was inscribed with "no worries" in about a dozen languages. Who knew that it would be so prescient!

Landmines made a lasting impression on me. I was at home in Ohio several months after this tour, and still remember flinching as my Mom drove over potholes. I did recognize that I was the problem and not Ohio potholes, but I think that was the beginning of my PTSD, one of the less appreciated souvenirs of my career.

When I finally drove to the embassy (after the land-mines were cleared), I noted a small tank parked facing the embassy's main entrance. The country's president had taken refuge in the U.S. embassy during a coup attempt, and the current regime did not want him going anywhere. Upon entry into embassy, I went directly into a meeting of key embassy personnel — all that remained at this mission, as any dependents and all "non-essential" personnel had already been evacuated from the post. The ambassador opened the meeting by stating that he was denying "country clearance" (permission to visit) to a U.S. Air Force colonel who could help with evacuation planning due to the current high danger level. My colorful thoughts included "how much worse can it get" along with . . . "so, what am I doing here?"

Still, I felt pretty safe at post thanks to the impressive ambassador Rusty Hughes, who had served as a Marine. His deputy was the somewhat eccentric, but also great, James Yellin, who was former Special Forces. He'd recently been out jogging by the golf course when a groundskeeper ran over a landmine. Fortunately neither was injured. James Yellin never gave up his jogging, and he later also served as ambassador to Burundi.

As to what I was doing in Burundi, the answer is "lots." The backlog of work was overwhelming as so many officers had been evacuated from post, and those who remained had other worries like stopping a potential civil war and trying to come up with a plan to reconcile our resident refugee president and the people responsible for the tank aimed at our embassy. My worst worry was that the embassy was regularly running out of the money it needed to function — or to pay to evacuate post if needed — but I quickly figured out and fixed that problem. If you have, say, a weekly budget of $1000 and essentials that used to cost thirty cents (my Snickers bar, for example) now cost $3, you'll burn through a budget pretty quickly. I drafted the justification to increase the post's operating funds, and got the authority to pay our local embassy staff in U.S. dollars instead of local currency. The local staff still had to deal with some inflation, but not the high level of inflation that left the local currency worthless.

Burundi is also where I supported efforts, including through advocacy at the international meeting mentioned in Chapter Two, to stop the killing and bring peace to this lovely country. Most Burundians I met were kind and compassionate: they were working for and deserved peace. The one official I met who advocated genocide as a solution to what he considered to be a "problem" of having citizens of differing opinions and appearances in the country, was not the norm.

My experience in Burundi reminded me of an incident from when I was traveling in Ireland years earlier, when Irish were killing Irish. As in Burundi, where years of intermarriage between Hutus and Tutsis had mingled populations, it could be difficult to tell who "the enemy" was. In Northern Ireland, I stayed with two delightful elderly ladies who ran a small bed and breakfast. When I paid my bill and accidentally used some money from the South, however, they began a vile diatribe against the "traitorous, treacherous scum of the South, who would be sure to foist their money off on me and cheat me at every opportunity." When I asked "but how do you know who's South and who's North," their immediate response was that "We Protestants spell Anne with an "e" while the Catholics spell it as "Ann." Really? Someone must have spent time and energy to come up with that ridiculous rule for hatred, time and energy that would have been better spent on kindness and reconciliation.

One personal observation and cautionary tale to any of you, dear readers, who might support a "just" war. Whatever the stated objectives or justifications, underlying rationales for war often come down to money and ego. Wars across Africa tended to be more ferocious and lasted longer when money was at stake, be it in proceeds from oil, diamonds or other commodities. And think of the U.S. involvement in war in Afghanistan. Over the 20 years of this war, the U.S. government has provided various rationales for the American military presence. It has not, however, managed to identify clear goals and a way forward to peace. It's easy to hype wars, but it takes courage, persistence, patience and *diplomacy* to avoid and to stop them.

Every assignment deserves a break, so I'll end here with notes from a trip back to the States for some sorely needed rest and relaxation (R&R). I loved playing in the snow (in summer) as my younger sister had saved snowballs in the freezer for me to offset my "snow deprivation syndrome." I also spent a week in Alaska, again, to counter snow deprivation. I knew some colleagues who — rather than be deprived of any of their interests — picked their assignments according to these interests. Thus, some of my colleagues only served in warm countries, or in Spanish-speaking countries, in those countries where they could surf or ski, or in those countries with beautiful music, arts, carpets, pottery . . . you name it. One memorable officer I worked with made sure he could go birding wherever he went, and I believe at one time held a world record for the number of different bird sightings he had recorded. Of course, we are better officers when we connect with the countries we work in, and art, artistry and music — among many other things — are wonderful connectors across cultures.

So join me on my break — get up, get a cup of tea, or get a brew — before we continue with more amazing adventures in Africa!

10

ROVING 'ROUND AFRICA
AFRICA, CONT., 1996-1998

So back to Africa, to **Kampala, Uganda**. This post was crazy for the two months I spent there to support the rare visit of a U.S. president to Africa, President Bill Clinton in 1998. My main job was tracking over 800 people from a dozen different U.S. government agencies, American and foreign media, and staff from about a dozen other U.S. embassies who supported the visit. My second job was finding them all places to stay, a bit difficult given that: the hotels weren't interested in kicking out long-term residents for the "privilege" of hosting these temporary visitors; the presidential advance team refused to guarantee payments for their rooms until I managed to convince them that without guarantees they'd be sleeping on the streets; and the number of rooms we needed didn't exist anyway. By the time the visit started, my spreadsheets identified about a million dollars' worth of rooms at 21 different establishments and hotels. I stayed at a flophouse, sorry, "guest house" on a cot, sharing a room with two other State Department officers. It worked out well since we were rarely in the room, and we were all too tired when we were there to notice if anyone snored. I did regret missed meals though: guest house meals were only available from 6:00-8:00 a.m. and 6:00-8:00 p.m. and I was never there for them. Fortunately, I'd packed a good stash of granola bars.

The presidential visit went well, and I was proud when White House staffers copied my "people tracker" spreadsheet, complete with cellphone numbers, arrival and departure dates and room assignments. After President Clinton departed, though, I discovered that some White House staffer had shut down the control room "because the president had left" — never mind that several hundred people still needed support to get out of town. I called Deputy Chief of Mission (later ambassador at several missions including Afghanistan) Michael McKinley. I advised him of the problem and explained that I was currently tracking down drivers, airport expeditors and other key people to fix it. And ok, I vented and asked him to read the White House staffer the riot act. The DCM arrived shortly afterwards with authority and a chocolate Easter bunny he'd taken from one of his children's Easter baskets for me. When he met up with me I'd just mediated and resolved the latest crisis: a total hotel blackout that the hotel was incorrectly blaming on us. One American technician who hadn't flown out of Kampala yet (and fortunately had a flashlight) graciously helped the hotel figure out their electrical issues. I enjoyed the Easter bunny as a great reward for extraordinary service, and as belated lunch and dinner on that 20-hour day. I would note that everyone successfully left town over the next few days.

The visit was rough, but both the DCM and U.S. ambassador to Uganda Nancy Powell were great. After weeks at my temporary quarters, I enjoyed the ambassador's hospitality at her official residence, which included fresh showers, my own bedroom and regular meals. I also enjoyed walking her dog occasionally, although I did worry that the nasty-looking-5-foot tall Marabou Storks (look them up!) in the neighborhood might snap up the puppy — or even me! After the president's departure, I was able to travel outside Kampala to see hippos, and the gorillas made famous in the film *Gorillas in the Mist.*

Ambassador Powell was creative and had a great sense of humor. She took me out to dinner on my final night in Uganda as thanks for a job well done. Joking with the owner, the ambassador mentioned that she wanted to make this event memorable. I responded that it would be hard to improve on the perfection that was the restaurant's trademark ice cream sundae. So the owner came out with perfection times two, a *double* ice cream sundae. I ate dessert first, fearing I'd be late for my flight out if I stayed for dinner, but managed a delicious dinner in the end.

Kinshasa, in the Democratic Republic of the Congo (DRC). The DRC is not to be confused with Republic of the Congo, the country right across the river from the DRC whose capital is Brazzaville. This will be important information later, when the shooting starts.

Kinshasa was another assignment with a not-your-normal entry on duty. I was met at the airport by an EFM, or Eligible Family Member. At a time of severe continuing personnel shortages, the State Department made good use of some of the amazing spouses of U.S. personnel posted at diplomatic missions. These spouses did work that kept missions running, covering jobs that would otherwise have gone unfilled. In this case, the State Department got a superbly qualified consular associate who was the sole American doing consular work at the mission. The Department didn't have to lobby her to come to this extreme hardship post or pay for her housing or any other costs here because she was already here with her officer husband. Meanwhile, she had professional work to keep her occupied and that would look good on a resume when she returned to the States.

At the airport, she asked me if I could accompany her on urgent consular business at the country's equivalent of the U.S. Department of Homeland Security. I quickly agreed. We met up with the mission's Defense Attaché and went to the Ministry where we were able to obtain the release of an American who had been unjustly imprisoned. Mind you, consular officers cannot normally get Americans out of jail. But in this instance, my colleague had done her homework and knew that the American had been illegally detained — and the host country had also already recognized this.

After a career in the U.S. military, this American citizen had returned to his birth country with the money to build a home for himself and his family. You will remember I've mentioned a certain lack of banks in Africa at this time? Well, the village chief apparently figured the American's hard-earned cash would be an easy target, robbed him, and then jailed him when he appeared on the chief's doorstep to get his money back. Word trickled in to the embassy and my colleague marshalled her resources to get the American released.

I helped on this case in a small way. I always travelled dressed for business so despite an agonizingly long flight and no time to clean up, I at least looked professional. I was introduced as "Stricker, from Washington" and the host country official's belief that "the detained American must have powerful connections" surely didn't hurt. But I must stress that the host government had already secured the American's release from the village chief before the embassy got involved.

In another clear example of this country's fight to overcome years of corruption and elite privilege under Mobutu Sese Seko, I give you the visa incident. My local staff was in a panic one day, noting that the current president's daughters were waiting patiently in line with other applicants for visas. Under the old regime, they would have bullied their way to the front of the line accompanied by armed thugs. Reestablishing rule of law and equal treatment for all was tough, but the Congolese were serious in their attempts to accomplish both.

Still, the country was not secure after years under the erratic, despotic former dictator. I returned to my hotel one day and it looked as if mortar fire had taken out the palm tree in the parking lot — where the parking lot attendant usually sat. I was pleased when the attendant reappeared several days later, shaken but fine. On another evening, I couldn't get back to the hotel through countless security cordons that had sprung up like mushrooms since I'd left for work that morning. After 20 minutes of trying to detour around them, I drove back to the embassy to see if the embassy's local national duty driver could get me home. He led on me on the same meanderings with a similar lack of success until suddenly pulling off the road into what seemed to be a chicken farm. Feathers flew, but I made it back to the hotel that night. And one leisurely afternoon I was watching a fire fight over the river — until I realized that a thin glass window offered no protection from stray rounds. I got a good book and sat in the sturdy bathtub in the bathroom at the rear of my hotel room until the shooting stopped.

Even scarier than the shooting was the apparent cause of the fire fight, and how easily a war could have started. I was told that the day of the shooting, someone on the Brazzaville side of the Congo River was trying to shoot fish.

Kinshasa troops thought they were being fired upon and fired back, and it looked pretty serious until wiser heads prevailed and stopped the shooting. I also learned that the security barriers of the chicken farm incident were due to reports of an attempted coup after a card game got out of hand and shots were fired near the presidential palace. And one day at my hotel, a teenaged "soldier" dropped his weapon in the lobby. Fortunately it didn't go off so no one shot back, but I'm sure several people had heart palpitations.

In the post-9/11 era, the State Department has taken a number of measures to improve employees' security overseas. It has enhanced the security of our facilities and housing, and significantly improved our personal security training. Both have been essential as diplomats have been targeted more frequently in these dangerous times. Bollards as barriers to defend against car bombs, window film that prevents shards of glass from serving as lethal weapons, and expanded security perimeters are just a few of the improvements that protect U.S. diplomats. We also receive focused anti-terrorism training, and participate regularly in drills to ensure we are prepared to handle any emergency. I privately had taken CPR and first responder training — and then was trained by the State Department as a chemical, biological and nuclear first responder at a post where loose nuclear and other hazardous materiel were major concerns.

I was assigned to U.S. Embassy **Lilongwe, Malawi** for just a few short weeks. Post was settled enough that U.S. Ambassador Ellen Shippy gave me and another temporary staffer a weekend off to travel to Victoria Falls. This was a relatively short (5 hour!) and direct flight to a spectacular site on the border between Zambia and Zimbabwe. I particularly appreciated her approving the journey, since it left the ambassador with few other Americans at this woefully understaffed mission.

My colleague and I had a wonderful weekend: we helicoptered over the falls, trekked everywhere, and had a memorable white water rafting adventure that began with the guide telling us to "jump out of the raft and into the river."[P11] We hesitated just a bit thinking about crocodiles, hippos and worse, but in the end, we all jumped into the river. Remember I talked about credibility? Well, the guide looked at us, said he was happy to have our trust — and that he now believed we would listen to him and stay safe on the trip. After this wonderful weekend off, we flew back to Lilongwe and were surprised to see a Diplomatic Security Officer from a neighboring embassy on our flight. He told us there had been a carjacking at a U.S. Information Service (USIS) event, and he'd been called to post to help police and the embassy with the crime scene and investigation. No American citizen died, but one foreign doctor I knew was killed and others injured. I spent some of my remaining days in Lilongwe working to enhance security at USIS.

Lome, in Togo, was hard-hit by staffing gaps, as noted in my evaluation that year: " . . . leave and illness exacerbated our problems, felling the backups to the backups. [Carol] served at times there as Admin., GSO and consular officer, acting PAO [public affairs officer], and represented the Ambassador in a ceremony presided over by the host country president." If I had ever, heaven forbid, had an accident, I would have had to get myself medical attention; authorize and sign off on the money to pay for it (illegally breeching regulations that do not permit the same officer to both authorize and spend funds); take care of any of my other concerns as a consular officer supporting my American Citizen Service needs; and then draft the press release to keep the host country informed. Fortunately I didn't need any of the above, but was able to provide all these services to the mission during my several weeks there.

Lome's exceptional Deputy Chief of Mission Terence McCulley (later ambassador to the Ivory Coast) surprisingly showed up in the consular offices one day, just as I was getting ready to handle a sensitive consular case. In non-diplomatic terms, this was a case in which I had to deny a well-connected Togolese a visa to the United States. The DCM was already aware of the case and took it upon himself to deny a visa to this applicant. He could have easily made me the fall guy, but instead took time from his packed schedule to deal with the difficulties, just one of many examples of his stellar support to his team. More importantly, it sent a clear signal to certain Togolese that U.S. Embassy Lome had strong and savvy leadership, and that it was a waste of time to try and "buy" a U.S. visa with money and influence. Had I denied the visa, the individual in question would have certainly worked his way up the chain of command to try and overcome this "bad decision by some junior officer who didn't realize who he was."

This incident is a good lead into what people within the State Department call "corridor reputation." I've described the U.S. Foreign Service's rigorous annual evaluations process, but admit that at times these could be inflated, or might overlook pertinent information about an officer. "Corridor reps," often corrected these deficiencies. People like the Lome DCM, and other senior officials I've mentioned by name were often so highly regarded that even if they were serving at extreme hardship posts, facing civil unrest, bombs and bullets, other officers rushed to volunteer to serve with them. Contrast that to poor leadership that made even some of the garden spots of Europe, for example, hard to staff.

Luanda in Angola was a lock-down post, too dangerous to even leave the guarded embassy compound. I lived in a trailer on this compound with a postage size swimming pool, and a treadmill in the mission's conference room. Amenities were sorely lacking, but I enjoyed one fabulous dinner (steak flown in from the States) hosted by an American oil company. I also shared one sentimental dinner of pizza from canned sauce, a carton (just add water) of dough, and dehydrated cheese thanks to a creative care package from my sister and my Mom that — yes — included their famous cookies.

Luanda took the "most scary moment" trophy, when what looked like to me like a Russian attack helicopter swooped down on the embassy compound as I was swimming. My life didn't flash before my eyes, but I had time to think "what the heck have we missed that they're attacking the embassy" and "hey, water is a good buffer, if I dive deep enough maybe the bullets won't get me." When I finally surfaced, I was told that helicopter hovering was a frequent violation of embassy airspace as the pilots checked out the female personnel in the pool.

Maputo in Mozambique was one of several posts I served at twice, and I was pleased to note significant improvements in the country when I returned a year after my first visit. On my first trip I was told to stay inside always, and I heard about embassy joggers whose running shoes were stolen — off their feet — the day before I arrived. I was also told of the wonderful restaurant overlooking the ocean that was constantly being robbed. It still served freshly caught seafood, but customers had to bring their own dishes and silverware. I did manage one wonderful outing during my first assignment to Maputo over the border to Kruger National Park in safer South Africa. I left with colleagues early Friday evening and returned early Sunday evening to avoid breaking curfew restrictions.

When I returned to Maputo the second time, I enjoyed full service at the seafood restaurant several times and spent a wonderful weekend on the beautiful Mozambican coast. The area was littered with landmines so we had to carefully stay on clearly marked paths, but tourism had a great future. It was thrilling to swim with dolphins, and I caught a ride on a whale shark, although in retrospect I'm not sure the guide should have said it was ok. These behemoths can be 60 feet (18 meters) long and weigh over 30 tons, so I'm sure it didn't notice me but this was its home turf. I was so excited that I was smiling like a fool — and foolishly sucked in a huge quantity of water when the whale shark suddenly dove. I just couldn't stop smiling or let go. That was one amazing life moment.

In Mozambique I enjoyed being able to use the Portuguese I'd learned as a high-school exchange student to Brazil. My older sister, in one of the many great care packages I received over the years from family, had included a Portuguese primer that helped me bone up on this language I had not used in years. My Portuguese came in handy when I had to talk the embassy's guards down from going on strike. The company for which they'd worked for years had gone out of business, taking their hard-earned pension benefits with them. The guards appreciated my efforts (as an "important person from Washington") to speak to them in Portuguese, and listened as I outlined the State Department's efforts to remedy the situation. They agreed not to strike at this high-security-threat post, and the State Department did send a check to compensate them and replace some of their pension funding.

Interestingly, I was long gone from post by the time the check arrived on the desk of my replacement, a rover colleague who featured in an earlier tale of airports and expeditors. He later told me that it was a bit of a shock to have this huge check hit his desk. But he knew what it was about due to the notes I'd left behind about the history and resolution of this major issue for whomever would follow me in Mozambique. He thanked me for both the notes — and for all the hard work that went into getting the check that helped address the problem.

Nouakchott, Mauritania was a short posting, just a few weeks long. I was able to address some fraud (the fact the local staffer would switch from French to Arabic when I came within hearing distance of his phone conversations was a huge hint that something was wrong); major consular and other backlogs; and provide the embassy the guidance and support it needed to maintain operations and move forward on a number of mission goals. This post seemed to me to be even more isolated than Timbuktu, with minimal infrastructure and almost nothing available in this desert capital. Camels roamed "downtown" and I don't remember many paved roads — traffic didn't seem to respect the roads anyway. I do remember the wonderful people of Mauritania who were so gracious and welcoming.

In Nouakchott, I had to commute to work in a sand-storm. I lived on the embassy compound, but couldn't see across the courtyard to my office. I shut my eyes, stuck out my arms and marched forward to the courtyard's opposite side. When I hit this wall a few minutes later, I followed along it until I felt the embassy door. I also recall, at this isolated mission with few amenities, painting a rainbow in a narrow stairwell that led to the tiny cellar room that was the embassy's commissary. I switched out a light fixture so people could actually see their way down the stairs, and more importantly, managed to obtain some real groceries to fill it.

When I arrived, there were only a few expired packages of junk food on otherwise empty shelves. My most treasured memory, though, was of the farewell beach party embassy employees held to thank me for my all my hard work. The beachfront setting for our picnic was spectacular, and we enjoyed it for a bit longer than expected as one of our vehicles got stuck in the sand.

In **Ouagadougou, Burkina Faso**, I served, often concurrently, as General Services Officer (GSO), head of personnel, and even as acting Deputy Chief of Mission. I never served as acting ambassador (Chargé) during my rover tour, but I often served with temporary duty Chargés due to the persistent and pervasive staffing gaps that continue today. Remember, dear reader, as I come to the end of this two-year tour dedicated to covering staffing gaps, that any time there are gaps, that means that work is not getting done. From the responsibilities of the first-tour GSO who is trying to keep the embassy running, to the first tour political officer who is reporting on issues that might need U.S. support — or action to help avoid potential problems — and up through and including the ambassador, the State Department has determined the staffing it needs to carry out the U.S. government goals for which it is responsible. Multiple and long-term staffing gaps mean that these goals are not being met. Vacancies at the ambassador level mean that U.S. embassies have lost crucial leadership capabilities and a powerful and influential voice in support of essential U.S. interests abroad.

In Ouagadougou I also served as duty officer for almost half my time there. Duty officers, you may recall from my Mali and Montreal stories, are the people who get called out of bed at 2:00 a.m. to handle emergencies — and I volunteered frequently to serve in that capacity. At the time, the only officer more senior or more experienced than I was the ambassador, who already had a full plate of responsibilities.

Ouagadougou reminded me of my foreign colleague in Washington's "fresh air smoking fiends" observation, and the lesson that one should never make assumptions. I was impressed to see what I thought was a thriving economy there, based on the many motorized mopeds and other vehicles in the streets driven by well-dressed riders. I quickly learned that most people were grossly indebted and that the current economy was not sustainable. At the embassy itself I was pleased to see several women who seemed to be very much respected in what was otherwise a male-dominated continent. Then I learned that one was royalty and another occupied a prestigious position in the embassy so they were respected *despite* their gender. Positive change was coming, though. Across Africa, U.S. diplomats were working with Africans and their governments — and making progress — on promoting democracy, enhancing security, supporting health initiatives and good education and expanding opportunities for all, including for women. I was proud to have been a part of those effort towards peace and prosperity, and continued those efforts in my next overseas assignment.

So please join me next in . . . Niamey, Niger.

11

NIGER AND THE TRAUMA OF TERRORISM
2000-2002

eptember 11, 2001. We all remember where we were on 9/11, the day that brought the havoc and heartache of terrorism home to the United States. I was in Niamey, Niger.

Terrorism had been my reality long before 9/11, from my time serving as a counterterrorism analyst to my decades as a diplomat. Diplomats are truly the first line of defense for the United States, keeping a host of ills away from the homeland. I had worked long, hard hours to make the world a better place and I'd particularly hoped to tackle terrorism at its roots by addressing poverty and hopelessness. I labored to keep bad people and bad things (terrorism, crime, disease) away from the United States. As a counterterrorism intelligence analyst, as a consular officer issuing visas, as a security officer overseas and by carrying out my other diplomatic duties, I helped keep the United States safe for a time. Overseas, however, terrorism was getting worse. In 1998, I lost friends and colleagues in the bombings at the U.S.

embassies in Nairobi, Kenya and Dar es Salaam, Tanzania. In 2000, in Niger, I lost a good friend in a carjacking. But — this was overseas, and I did not want my reality to be yours.

Then came 9/11, and it changed our world forever. On the home front we now watch for unattended packages on public transportation, worry about mass shootings and bombings, and fear flying home for the holidays as airports and airplanes have become terrorists' targets of opportunity. For diplomats abroad, it has made our work even more difficult. Today we are truly in a war against terror, a war in which we have to be perfect and protect and defend against every threat, every day — while the terrorists only have to get it right once.

The very basics of diplomacy have been negatively affected. A diplomat needs to get out of what can easily become a protected embassy "bubble" to meet the people in the country to which they are assigned. In my years overseas, I joined in activities and did things I'd never imagined I would to better connect with people, and as a reality check on the "official" party line and my more rarified experiences as a "dignitary." My homes in every country were havens for visiting U.S. Peace Corps Volunteers who lived far from the big cities, and provided vastly different perspectives on the countries in which we lived.

I made efforts to reach out in every assignment. I visited orphanages and talked to prisoners. I talked to bank tellers, gas station attendants, farmers, and the women starting up micro-enterprises that gained them dignity and independence in male-dominated societies. I went into the classrooms to talk to students and teachers, made heart-wrenching visits to local hospitals, and as a consular officer visited U.S. citizens in foreign prisons. People told me that I was the first diplomat they had ever met. I made sure I left people with a positive impression, that I was a thoughtful, gracious American and a normal human being with whom they could connect.

These experiences helped me do my job better, and helped the mission as I shared my findings with my embassy colleagues. I remember talking with one officer about rampant racism in one country, a racism which he'd never noticed as a white male. I mentioned an Asian American Peace Corps Volunteer who left the country before his tour ended. He was tired of children throwing sticks and rocks at him while calling out, "Jet Li, Jet Li," and expecting him to burst into kung fu moves to protect himself. A realistic view of this racism was appropriately reflected in the embassy's annual human rights review on the country.

I mentored new officers and helped them learn the value of venturing out beyond the embassy walls. When I arrived in Niger, six of the eight Americans I supervised — on that rare occasion when we were fully staffed — were first-tour officers, and several had little or no overseas experience. To help them and their family members overcome culture shock, become familiar with, and successfully work and live in this demanding environment, I created the "Road Rally/Scavenger Hunt." After 9/11, diplomatic vehicles racing around any nation's capital would have been seen as some terrible security crisis.

The Hunt included directions and clues to important locations in town such as the local market, a grocery store and the Marines' Residence. Back in the "olden days" when missions were truly isolated, the Marines obtained first-run movies which were originally on film and then on video-tapes and dvds. They continue this tradition today with their always popular movie nights.

The Hunt's winning team was the one that finished the course the fastest, *and* had figured out the most clues.

There were also challenges along the way, one of which required the team to bargain at the market for the "biggest bang for a buck" award. The winner of this award was a spouse on her first trip overseas. As she reported back, she had no idea *what* she had bought, but she managed to get the message across in limited French — with internationally understood arm gestures — that she wanted the biggest bunch of whatever product she could get. More importantly, she came back knowing that she could make herself understood and succeed with the hospitable people in this new environment.

One team won the "Mud Cloth," award, which was a beautiful piece of traditional fabric that had been dyed with wet clay (thus "mud" cloth) and natural plants. I'm not sure where they'd been in this desert country, but their vehicle had waist-high mud marks on it. Another team could have earned a "creativity" award. Shortly into the game, I overheard them using the embassy radio net to ask the embassy motor pool drivers for help with some of the navigation clues. I cut in to let them know we could hear them — but later commended their ingenuity at the Hunt's award banquet. I let everyone know that the embassy emergency radio system could be an invaluable resource in case of a flat tire or other problem on the road.

I also ran in several countries with the Hash House Harriers, a running club started by, as fellow runners happily told me "eccentric Brits." Basically, a member will mark a trail (usually using chalk or flour), which may include dead ends, false trails and other tests of observational skills and endurance. The hares (the fastest runners) often run twice as far as slower participants, but everyone winds up together at the end because the slower participants, noticing the hares coming back from the false trails, don't waste their time and effort going down them. Today, security concerns in many countries would prevent this and many other public activities. In Frankfurt, Germany (my assignment after Niamey), trick-or-treating was cancelled: masked people running around the embassy compound were a security concern. And in Tbilisi (after Frankfurt), I served at one of the U.S. "fortress embassies" designed and built after 9/11 to better protect U.S. mission personnel. These embassies were often far from city centers and thus difficult to get to and enter into due to security measures. In short, they kept people away.

In addition to terrorism and an inexperienced — but impressive — staff, the U.S. embassy in Niger faced a host of other challenges. Niger was one of the poorest countries in the world, with little infrastructure, unreliable Internet, a poorly educated population and poor health services. The embassy suffered from such severe and long-term staffing gaps that I covered two to five positions concurrently for my entire tour. I was assigned as Management Officer. I also served almost a year as Human Resources Officer with added responsibilities for the U.S.embassy in neighboring Burkina Faso, and several months each as General Services and Budget Officers. As post's Acting Security Officer I was the institutional memory for seven temporary security officers during their short visits to this country sandwiched between Libya and Nigeria, with rising regional tensions and increasing security concerns. I served almost six months as the Acting Deputy Chief of Mission, including during 9/11, and as Acting Ambassador (Chargé). Six of my American staff were new to their jobs, and the local staff was also under strength, with new personnel. It was a full-time job to fill vacancies, give everyone the training and tools they needed to learn their jobs and do them well and to address the mismanagement and fraud that resulted from previous staffing gaps. The work was worth it, however, as the new team that resulted was great and able to handle anything this challenging environment threw at them.

I would have had to cover a four-month-long backlog in visa issuances, too, a backlog that had become a contentious public issue in Niger. Fortunately, I was able to use my credibility and contacts in Washington to bring out a remarkable woman from Washington who cleared the backlog in weeks. I brought in an outstanding Foreign Service National (FSN) warehouse manager from a neighboring post, too, to close down our numerous storage sheds scattered around Niamey and consolidate them into a one organized warehouse. Within weeks, the warehouse project was done, and we had a computerized inventory system that enabled us to track stock and order what we needed to keep the Embassy running. This was important in Niger, as it could take a year or more to get supplies in from overseas. I brought another brilliant FSN from a neighboring post to train my new procurement staff, after firing several employees for the fraud they committed during years of poor oversight and staffing gaps. By the time the visiting expert left, the fraud was fixed, a year's backlog in bills and problems addressed, and the new procurement team was working well. Finally, I spend time at U.S. Embassy Ouagadougou, clearing out an almost year-long backlog of personnel actions including delayed promotions and pay raises that were hurting mission morale.

Expertise matters in any environment. Experts get it right the first time, avoid pitfalls, and work at maximum efficiency. I'm embarrassed, here in the United Sates, when I need to deal with a company several times to fix one issue. When a company errs, it's bad for business, and wastes my time and theirs. It is unprofessional, costs them the salaries of staff who have to handle the same issue so many times — and costs them the customers who leave for better service and products. Expertise can be expensive, but it's cheaper than the alternative and saves valuable time, money and reputations.

My work was recognized through awards from the State Department's Bureau of African Affairs, and kudos from the Office of the Inspector General (OIG). Three things were, however, even more important to me than this recognition: 1) the positive feedback I'd received from my staff and the entire mission team; 2) that we met our mission goals that included fostering democracy and fighting against terrorism; and 3) that the embassy would be able to continue this good work even after I left post.

I left Embassy Niamey with a strong team. Yet, lack of expertise coupled with staffing gaps remain a problem at too many U.S. diplomatic missions. Many of the problems I dealt with arose — or were made worse — by staffing gaps. Problems not dealt with do not go away but instead fester and grow bigger. The United States and its people deserve a State Department that is adequately funded and staffed so it can fulfill its responsibilities for U.S. strategic national interests. In return, the State Department remains accountable to the American people for the programs and personnel that U.S. tax dollars fund: the State Department is subject to full audits annually, and to periodic inspections as needed.

In my various assignments, I worked long hours and used my expertise to improve the State Department's ability to carry out this mission to defend the United States, its people and its interests. In Niger, I feared that my expertise and hard work would not be enough. In Niger, I served for months in either the number two position at the embassy (as Deputy Chief of Mission), or as the Acting Ambassador (Chargé). I give you one example of the difference between being the official ambassador appointed by the President and confirmed by the Senate, and being chargé.

As Chargé, I was called on a secure phone from a U.S. military representative asking for intelligence on my country for an imminent U.S. military operation in it. This was at a time of the growing U.S. military presence in the world, and a troubling tendency to look for "quick" military fixes instead of diplomacy to deal with problems. Did you know that the U.S. military operates in dozens of countries worldwide? They were operating in Niger — above and beyond the Defense Attaché Office — when I was Chargé, and I did not know it.

A January 2019 *Smithsonian Magazine* article reveals that the U.S. military now operates in 40% of the world's nations.[40] As ambassador, I could have questioned a U.S. military operation there, and made sure they coordinated properly with the host country to gain better intelligence and ensure the safety of the personnel involved. As Chargé, I didn't feel I had the authority to raise questions. I stressed that the region concerned was a hotbed of criminality and bad behavior and counseled that they should prepare for the worst. Fortunately, no-one died on my watch. In contrast, a February 2018 *New York Times* article "'An Endless War': Why 4 U.S. Soldiers Died in a Remote African Desert" tells the story of a military operation with the more tragic loss of U.S. life that I had feared.[41]

In the Trump administration, 50 ambassadorships — out of about 190 — were vacant at one point. And over 40% of the first ambassadors appointed by this administration were political appointees, without the years of experience and expertise in foreign affairs that career ambassadors have.[42]

According to the American Foreign Service Association, the professional organization of America's diplomats, countries that had no ambassador for over two years included Egypt, Jordan, Qatar, Cuba, Honduras, Panama and Brazil. Other vacancies were in multinational organizations such as the Organization of American States which covers much of Latin America and deals with immigration and other important issues, and the Organization for Economic Cooperation and Development which supports market economies across the world to promote economic growth, prosperity and sustainable development.

The United States cannot be a global leader when we have vacancies in so many leadership positions. Without a strong presence in these countries and organizations, we will miss many opportunities to work productively with like-minded allies on issues including terrorism, pandemics, food insecurity and climate change. I wrote earlier that forfeiting global leadership — to China for example — should be a strategic decision and not the inadvertent result of budget cuts. Forfeiting global leadership should also not be the result of staffing gaps, or of filling our leadership positions with people who do not have the qualifications needed to lead. Absent U.S. leadership, U.S. strategic national interests cannot be advanced and protected.

My duties in Niger included providing support to the OIG inspection team and over 250 other visitors to Niger during my two years there. I handled legal cases ranging from a class-action lawsuit against the embassy to a diplomatic flap over U.S. diplomatic pouches that a host country official demanded to open in violation of international law. I also had to — quoting directly from my annual evaluation — "Convince the government of Niger to sign a Full Safeguards Agreement on uranium." Niger, the world's third-largest uranium producer and second-poorest country in the world, could have decided to supply neighboring Libya and other terrorism-supporting countries with nuclear material for fast cash. I did advocacy on this issue, which included more démarches in French.

As in every assignment, I know that I made a difference in Niger and I enjoyed my tour. One unique adventure involved traveling to the Niger's northern desert to support the University of Chicago's Dr. Paul Sereno on his expedition to research a 112-million-years-old old 40-foot long crocodile skeleton (dubbed SuperCroc) that he had discovered there.[P12] I visited Agadez, a World Heritage Site and major trading center from the 15th century, which was one of the most fascinating cities I've ever seen. I attended a Tuareg festival too, complete with camel races, feats of skill and dancing. The Tuareg, also know as the "Blue Men of the Desert" for the indigo dyes of their turbans and robes, are among the last remaining nomadic tribes on Earth.

One sad duty in Niger though, was dealing with a personal tragedy due to terrorism. In Niger I supported the re-opening of our Defense Attache Office (DAO), which worked to de-politicize and professionalize the country's military. When the head of our DAO office was killed and our Marine Security Guard Detachment Commander injured in a terrorist carjacking, the entire embassy went into shock — but also swung professionally into crisis management mode.

DAO chief Bill Bultemeier was one of the good guys who spent his life — often in harm's way — trying to make the world a better place. He did it with humor: in our last conversation he joked, "What have you done for me lately?" I reminded him that I'd managed to get his official vehicle through customs so he could now shave in the car's rear-view mirror. I also promised him that I would never give up the search for that impossible-to-find-in-town regular bathroom mirror. We both laughed. Bill was also the classic "can do" American. Shortly after I met him, we were on a sweltering airport tarmac with an injured American waiting for a long-overdue medical evacuation flight. In this country with no vending machines or fast food outlets, Bill managed to scrounge drinks and snacks to keep us all hydrated and fed.

When Bill was killed, the entire Embassy was heartbroken, but we knew that we had to take care of him as well as he had taken care of us. This was difficult, as all of our DAO institutional memory went with him. I recall talking to U.S. military personnel in other countries, and they weren't quite sure how to call me at my non-military phone number — and couldn't explain how I could call them from a non-military phone. Regular phone lines I'd called on were static-ridden and sometimes failed. The U.S. military crew for the evacuation flight was worried too, about flying into Niamey, possibly over prohibited airspace. Fortunately I was able to handle the institutional issues, including keeping the U.S. military flight out of proscribed air space.

At the same time, we were caring for Christopher McNeely, the Marine Security Detachment Commander who was shot as he dove to cover Bill and help him. Embassy team members coordinated with local police and security to gather crime scene evidence, and worked with the hospital, local authorities, government officials and U.S. authorities in Europe and Washington. By the end of that first 20-hour day, we'd done what was needed to get Christopher and his family to the U.S military hospital in Landstuhl Germany and to send Bill's remains home. The embassy Marines even did a stealth run to load the evacuation plane with the gifts

Christopher's children were able to open in Germany on Christmas morning, although their father's successful surgery was the best gift of all. Throughout the Christmas holiday, everyone pitched in to deal with this terrible tragedy.

Justice was finally served 16 years later. In 2016, Bill's killer was convicted of murder in a New York court and sentenced to 25 years in prison.[43]

I remember the good will of the Nigeriens who came up to me after the killing to offer their support and condolences and to emphasize that these killings did not represent Niger. I was at the embassy in Niger on September 11, 2001, and again remember the extraordinary outpouring of support for the United States in this Muslim country. We squandered an opportunity for positive change by not committing at that time to a fight with the Nigeriens against the terrorism that targeted us both.

Two years after my arrival in Niger this extraordinary tour of duty ended and I moved on to my next assignment in Frankfurt, Germany.

12

ROVER TOUR ON STEROIDS
AKA GOOD GOVERNMENT
FRANKFURT, GERMANY, 2002-2004

In 2002, I was assigned to the U.S. Consulate Frankfurt, Germany, as the Deputy Director of the Frankfurt Regional Support Center (RSC). The consulate at the time was the U.S. government's fifth largest diplomatic mission and a powerhouse of interagency and international coordination. As Deputy Director, I took full advantage of the RSC's synergies and experts to train, outfit, and support dozens of U.S. diplomatic missions across the globe so they, in turn, could efficiently and effectively advance U.S. government goals worldwide. Remember my road trip from Embassy Kiev to the RSC to get supplies to outfit that new mission? Now I was the one filling requests for resources, support and training for missions, including U.S. Embassies Baghdad and Kabul. This was an incredible chance to have an enduring impact on State's ability to carry out its core mission: to create a more secure, democratic and prosperous world for the benefit of the American people and the global community.

This job was a perfect assignment based on my career to date: I'd been in the field, knew policy and plans from a Washington perspective and knew what was needed to accomplish both. The timing was perfect, too, as we now had Secretary of State Colin Powell, a leader who focused not just on policy, but also on the tools, training and personnel we needed to do our jobs and make policy happen. Secretary Powell's efforts to improve our security at posts around the world were also appreciated after the 1998 bombings of our embassies in Nairobi and Dar es Salaam. As with all my previous jobs, however, there were wrinkles. Some were anticipated, some not, and most were due to years of pervasive staffing gaps.

For years, the State Department had not hired enough people even to replace those who retired or otherwise left the service. Remember, I covered more than one job at every post I'd ever worked at, and I was not unique. With Secretary Powell's Diplomatic Readiness Initiative, the State Department hired almost 1,800 new people in one year alone — and funded the training needed for *all State* Department personnel. Another important metric: In 2000, only 2% of State personnel had access to the Internet. In contrast, almost half of American households had Internet in 2000, while academics had been using the Internet for years. A good overview of the sad "state of State" can be found in a November 2003 article on "Powell's Army" in *Government Executive* magazine.[44] Thanks to Secretary Powell, by the end of 2002 over 50% of employees had Internet access, classified systems were upgraded — and people had the computer training they needed to use these and other new tools.

Still, many more people needed more training immediately: on computers and other new tools, on programs, policies and substantive matters, and on leadership and management. In this "Rover Tour on Steroids" I could, if careful and creative, meet the needs of the people I had to support. I helped veteran officers who were suddenly managing large offices without the management training or experience they needed. I helped the new officers who were frequently posted to small, isolated hardship posts without the experienced mentors and bosses who could help them succeed — and I helped everyone in between.

In Frankfurt, I had to help U.S. missions world-wide. The first wrinkle to hinder this goal was, as you might guess, that in Frankfurt we didn't have sufficient personnel, adequate facilities or the core materials needed to train everyone immediately. Second: No matter how well you train someone, experience, particularly field experience, is also needed. We provided prioritized, targeted training in a "just-in-time" sort of assembly line to those needing it most, although I often fantasized about a sci-fi future in which we could plug people into computers and dump the data and other input needed directly into their brains. A third — and unexpected — wrinkle came in early 2003, after the United States invaded Iraq and overthrew Saddam Hussein's regime. To help address Iraq's many challenges, U.S. Embassy Baghdad expanded exponentially, taking in many of the new hires who otherwise would have gone to fill persistent staffing gaps elsewhere. The RSC sent its own staff to Baghdad, trained staff going to Baghdad, and developed and supported "virtual" work in budget, personnel and other areas so people didn't need to go to Baghdad or other danger zones, but could still accomplish the work that need to be done to support these U.S. missions.

My job as Deputy Director of the Regional Support Center had four main components. The first was to liaise with posts to determine their supply needs and then coordinate with the U.S. military to meet those needs through military surplus. As U.S. military facilities down-sized or closed after the fall of the Soviet Union, we used their surplus resources to build up diplomatic posts. We provided everything and anything to posts across Europe, and even to our growing missions in Iraq and Afghanistan. Remembering the polluted parking lot where U.S. Embassy Kiev children played, I was pleased to be able to deliver playground equipment in response to one enterprising post's request.

A second component was working creatively with IT specialists and trainers to develop teleworking — and to train people on this relative novelty in 2002. This was crucial for Embassy Baghdad and other hardship posts, because it helped us reduce staff in these dangerous places while still maintaining quality service. It was also helpful in small posts, from which complicated budget or other work could be sent to experts at regional centers. Having a "virtual" budget officer ensured sound financial management and helped avoid any potential waste, fraud or mismanagement that could occur with inexperienced or overwhelmed personnel. We also fostered standardization so that officers moving from one post to the next didn't have the steep learning curve that I had in my rover tour. To the extent possible, things were now done the same way from Albania to Zimbabwe.

A third component addressed posts' training needs so that the people, particularly in our newly-established posts, could quickly get up to speed and do their jobs as effectively as possible. To determine needs — from the basics and beyond of political and consular tradecraft, to how to run a warehouse — we kept in close touch with the Office of the Inspector General (OIG), the regional bureau offices in Washington, the Foreign Service Institute (FSI), which is the State Department's premier training institution, and posts themselves. We paid particular attention to the OIG inspection reports, reviewing them for recurring weaknesses and other matters that could be addressed with targeted training.

The Foreign Service Institute in Washington kept abreast of changes in policies and procedures and developed an incredible array of courses to help people in the field deal with these changes. In Frankfurt, we were a force magnifier for FSI, bringing training to people in the field who otherwise might not have received critical training — or received it years after it was needed. The regional bureaus and posts themselves also weighed in on training needs, covering problems that surfaced *between* regularly scheduled OIG visits.

Much of the RSC training consisted of live classes held at the Frankfurt RSC facility itself. We had some amazing experts on staff, including one FSI instructor — a Civil Service employee on a special assignment to Frankfurt for two years to help ensure that we met the State Department's professional training standards. It was much cheaper to bring dozens of American and local national staff to Germany than to pay for them to travel back to Washington for training.

We also sent trainers to our diplomatic missions. One outstanding group of trainers was the Foreign Service National Corps, which was composed of foreign nationals from various U.S. missions. Chosen for their expertise, these local staffers put aside their own duties once or twice a year to provide training to other posts. Again, the cost effectiveness of sending one person to a neighboring post to train a dozen or more people and to provide an on-site operations review and guidance, was considerable. Further, the foreign national trainers often spoke the same language as the staff they were training, and unlike American officers who moved on to other jobs after a few years, they could serve as permanent mentors to their trainees. Their service was priceless.

The final component of my job was travel. My staff and I regularly visited our core 40 (former Soviet Union and other) posts, as well as posts that needed an extra assist after major staffing gaps, loss of personnel or other concerns. The visits were a mix of looking for weaknesses, and providing timely assistance and focused training.

Travel provided some memorable moments. After one late arrival in dangerous Tajikistan, there was, oddly, no expediter to meet me. I arrived at my hotel safely: armed guards everywhere discouraged crime, and my taxi had brakes, a floor and most of its other parts. To stay "medically safe," I stopped by the hotel gift shop to buy bottled water — but then decided against buying a "sealed " bottle that had clearly been opened and then refilled with the same muddy water available from local faucets. I finger-brushed my teeth that night and went to bed thirsty.

Armed guards at the front of the hotel provided a sense of security until I looked out from my room's window. My first-floor room at the back of the hotel was separated from an alley — filled with Friday night partiers coming from and going to a bar one block down the street — by a low wire fence that a kindergartener could have jumped over. More stressful to me was the palm-sized spider I found in my bathtub. I was exhausted and so deferred to the spider that night, putting a towel across the bathroom threshold so it couldn't get to me. It had disappeared by morning, so I was able to shower before heading into the office.

My side-trips to Samarkand and Bukhara, both UNESCO World Heritage Sites on the old "Silk Road" to China, were incredible. Thanks to limited flights in the region, I had a weekend to spend in Tashkent after finishing up an embassy review and training visit. I hired a driver and vehicle and enjoyed an exhausting but unforgettable sight-seeing opportunity. I visited Samarkand, one of the oldest cities in the world, with its amazing Islamic architecture and beautiful mosques. I then moved on to Bukhara, which was a significant religious center for centuries. In both, it was easy to imagine life centuries ago when caravans transported gold, silk and other riches between the West, including the Roman Empire, and China.[P11]

While in Frankfurt, I also enjoyed being in the same country with my brother serving in the U.S. military. I visited him several times, and even managed to attend his (due to service needs frequently postponed) wedding. A second brother came out with his wife and family to visit me, and we had a delightful tour of Germany and also toured Paris and Normandy. I've mentioned some of the care and care packages I received from my family, and help with shopping and other support from them. Going above and beyond, my sister-in-law actually "operated" on me during this trip. Shortly into the visit, I realized that I had some stitches on my back "left-over" from mole removal after a trip to the doctor to check for skin cancer after my years in Africa. My sister-in-law confirmed that the cuts were healed, then took my Swiss army knife and removed the stitches without blinking. Just one more example of the outstanding support my family gave me — and a reflection upon the creativity and can-do attitude that my family instilled in me that helped me so much in my wild career. It was a sad day, though, when security requirements at airports meant that I could no longer carry my beloved Swiss army knife everywhere. It had been so useful so often.

Two final notes on travel. First, some of my core personnel were on the road for most of their Frankfurt assignments. Still, one intrepid roving officer also spent her *free* time traveling. She hung out at the Frankfurt airport — one of the world's largest — waiting for the last-minute inexpensive tickets that airlines used to fill their planes. She would weekend in the Bahamas, or head up to Reykjavik to enjoy its hot springs or see the Northern Lights. Personally, I enjoyed the delights of travel closer to home, and loved the open borders and common currency (the newly introduced Euro) that made travel so much easier than when I was a student in Europe years earlier.

Second, and most importantly, even with our travel costs, the RSC was an excellent bargain for the State Department. In 2002, the Office of Management and Budget, (OMB) which reviews federal agencies for how effectively they spend federal funds, estimated that the average cost of having one full-time direct-hire American family of four in a U.S. embassy was $339,100.[45] Costs would be higher for dangerous posts such as Baghdad and Kabul due to additional security expenses. The RSC, with eight American and four Locally Engaged Staff — the new term for what were previously known as "Foreign Service Nationals" — provided expert service to our 40 core posts and dozens of additional ones for a cost of less than $3 million annually. This was a fraction of the $13.5 million it would have cost to assign a single officer to each of the "core 40" posts we supported. It would have cost even more for full staffing, as our officers often covered the duties of more than one officer at each post.

The RSC provided "just-in-time" expert service, continuing online service — particularly in financial and personnel management — and helped posts avoid the waste, fraud and mismanagement that I'd seen too often in understaffed and overwhelmed posts during my Africa Rover tour. The money the RSC saved the U.S. government was significant. Our support also helped avoid employee burnout, and as such was priceless. I was proud to be able, through good management and effective use of a growing array of online tools, to more than double the number of posts we helped during my two-year tour. Posts' thanks, praise from the Office of the Inspector General for helping posts meet critical U.S. government goals more efficiently and effectively, and knowing that I was saving the U.S. government money (I'm a taxpayer too!) while helping reduce staff at dangerous missions made all my hard work worthwhile.

But, on to that *unexpected* wrinkle. The Management Officer for the Frankfurt Consulate retired six months before the end of his tour and I was asked to fill his position. Overnight, I became responsible for the management of (quoting my evaluation for the period) "a full spectrum of administrative support provided to approximately 800 personnel, several hundred dependents, and 7 facilities" at this fifth-largest US diplomatic mission in the world." I oversaw a $50 million dollar budget, seven offices including budget, personnel, IT and medical, and liaised with and provided assistance to over two dozen independent U.S.G. agencies also located in Frankfurt. I also spent considerable time providing input and support to an $80 million project to consolidate all seven of the consulate's facilities scattered across Frankfurt at a former WWII-era U.S. military (surplus!) hospital.

These were my "regular duties," to which were added security and other responsibilities due to the Iraq War. I did contingency planning for evacuees coming to Frankfurt from other posts, given that so many of them travelled from Africa, the former Soviet Union and beyond through Frankkfurt's huge international airport. I also helped move one consulate office located away from the main consulate complex to a more secure location — and then back to the original office — after the threat level was reduced and the security at the original location upgraded.

There were also hundreds of officials visitors to deal with: in just one week I escorted a Supreme Court justice, an assistant secretary and several other high-level officials, and I was constantly hosting representatives from, or respond-ing to, inquiries from the Government Accountability Office (GAO), members of Congress, congressional staffers and others on a wide range of issues. I never dropped a ball, but I did drop communications once for a meeting with a high-level military/Congressional delegation returning from Afghanistan. Not quite awake when I pulled myself together for a very early morning arrival, I grabbed what I though was my cellphone off the counter. I was surprised when I tried to call someone later to find my travel alarm clock of the same size, shape and color in my purse instead of my cellphone. Oops!

As mentioned earlier, Frankfurt also had growth and staffing gaps to deal with, despite being such a large and well-established post. Many U.S. government agencies looked to expand their Frankfurt presence to provide remote virtual — or traveling regional — support to their personnel at other missions. These agencies, too, faced staff-ing gaps as they lost personnel who were needed to staff the rapidly growing U.S. Embassy in Baghdad. I personally had no deputy or office manager. Thankfully, I was able to partially cover these two vacant positions by hiring an incredibly capable spouse of one of the officers at post. With her superb support, we actually made progress on our over-whelming workload. My short commute (a 5-minute-walk across the U.S. government compound) meant I could also spend more time on the job. I did often have to answer a recurring question from other residents of the compound who saw my office lights on from 7a.m to 9 p.m.: "Do you live at the office?" I just reminded them I was working for them and they'd laugh. I felt appreciated, though, as people occasionally dropped by to say "hey," and to bring me cookies or other treats — and once even dinner!

A note on meetings is warranted here, as I spent a lot of time in Frankfurt in good ones. As you now know, embassies are run by ambassadors. The ambassador at every post generally chairs a weekly "Country Team" meeting, that gathers the key officers of all agencies and offices at post to discuss priorities, plans and issues, *and to ensure efficiency, effectiveness and coordination.* In Frankfurt, this meant that various U.S. agencies that were countering terrorism, drug and human trafficking and addressing other issues of serious national security concerns all had a seat at the table. They shared best practices, disturbing new trends and used their combined expertise to tackle challenges.

In just one example of a targeted meeting in Frankfurt on narcoterrorism: the Drug Enforcement Agency (DEA) might lead off, with representatives from the U.S. military, the Department of Homeland Security's Immigration and Customs offices and the Treasury Department. The Secret Service, which has been investigating and preventing the counterfeiting that bankrolls crime since it was created in 1865, would also be present, as would someone from the State Department's Bureau of International Narcotics and Law Enforcement Affairs. Consular officers, who work to track and stop criminals and terrorists trying to illegally cross borders, would also be present. Representatives from these differing U.S. government agencies also coordinated and met with their counterparts from the host country or even international agencies such as INTERPOL. I can't emphasize enough that working collectively, including with international partners, is the only way to address global issues such as terrorism, climate change, food insecurity, refugees, pandemics and so many more. Diplomats work with all interested parties on these issues, and America, Americans and the world are safer thanks to their efforts.

Smaller, isolated posts held good meetings too. In one African country, I attended the deputy chief of mission's monthly meeting with both the country team (including USAID and Peace Corps), and counterparts from other countries' diplomatic missions as well as non-governmental organizations such as Cooperative for Assistance and Relief Everywhere (CARE) and Oxfam. Together, the group decided on priorities, focusing on the most urgent needs that could realistically be addressed given existing resources and providing the "biggest bang for buck." Attendees then divided and conquered. They determined plans of action on each topic, and each person at the table made a commitment of time, money or resources that they had to avoid duplication of effort and to magnify the impact of each agency. Together, group members had a major and positive impact on the host country.

But — back to Frankfurt, where things happened that even the best meetings and brainstorming couldn't anticipate. Just before the Easter weekend as many businesses were closing, I received a call from our consular section regarding an anxious American whose U.S.-government-employee husband had been evacuated from an isolated post to Frankfurt and was being prepped for urgent surgery.

At that time, unfortunately, Americans in many countries were considered scofflaws who either didn't pay their medical bills (skipping town), or who had insurance agencies who paid after so much delay and trouble that they weren't worth taking on as patients. Today, the State Department recommends that all travelers carry travel insurance which pays medical costs upfront. In 2003 in Frankfurt, the surgeon prepping for the surgery discovered that his patient was an American and was demanding thousands of dollars upfront before he'd operate. Needless to say, the wife did not have thousands in cash on her.

I was able to confirm the patient's U.S. government employment status and figured out how to get the wife the money she needed. I had the wife (with checkbook!), catch a cab to the consulate from the hospital, and cash the check (that I'd pre-approved) at the consulate's cashier. In those security conscious days after 9/11, I also alerted post's security officer that a cab would be sitting near the consulate for the 20 minutes it would take me to meet the woman, escort her to the cashier's office, and then get her back to the cab so she could return to the hospital. The cab driver wasn't arrested as a potential car bomber, the wife made it back to the hospital with cash in time for her husband to be operated on — and I later received word that the surgery was successful and the patient was expected to make a full recovery.

Life in Frankfurt was never dull, and I was proud of the positive, enduring impact I had there. Efficiently — and cost effectively — I helped the State Department and other agencies create a more democratic, secure and prosperous world.

But now for a change of pace, as I move on to my next assignment in Tbilisi, in the former soviet Republic of Georgia.

13

"DEZHAVYU" — OR DÉJÀ VU
SOVIET STYLE
TBILISI, GEORGIA, 2004-2006

I was assigned as a management officer to U.S. Embassy Tbilisi in 2004, nine years after I'd left Ukraine and 13 years after Georgia declared independence from the Soviet Union. Georgia was more isolated and poorer than Ukraine. Further, It did not get the early and intense Western focus and assistance that Ukraine and its nuclear arsenal received. By the time I arrived, though, Tbilisi was getting international attention and the U.S. embassy was growing rapidly and supporting Georgia on a wide range of issues. Meanwhile, Georgians themselves were energized after their January 2004 election of pro-Western president Mikael Saakashvili, and the government was moving forward on strengthening its institutions, rule of law, anti-corruption efforts and other key goals.

Georgia had many of the same challenges that Ukraine had. These included numerous government shake-ups and legislation being written or revised weekly; weak institutions;

poor infrastructure; and a legacy of corruption from Soviet times. Russia also continually targeted Georgia's economic and political affairs, its Internet discourse and civil society as it tried to undermine Georgia's ties to the West and its attempts to build a strong democracy. In January 2006, during one of Georgia's coldest winters on record, explosions cut the Russian gas pipelines exporting gas to Georgia, leaving the Georgians literally out in the cold. Georgians, and many others, believed this incident was no accident. Georgia also had to deal with continuing Russian interference in Ossetia and Abkhazia. In 2008, the Russian military occupied these two regions despite United Nations and world-wide condemnation.

U.S. Embassy Tbilisi grew from 350 people to over 650 in five years, so most of my Georgian staff was new. Nine of the 14 Americans who reported to me were on their first or second tours, and many of the other Americans at post at that time also had little overseas experience with the U.S. government. With new agencies such as the Millennium Challenge Corporation (established the year I arrived in Tbilisi with a mandate to help wean governments off foreign aid), even the U.S. agency heads had a learning curve.

In addition, the embassy's physically separated facilities were impediments to good supervision and oversight. The difficult Georgian language that I couldn't speak or read made me appreciate earlier assignments where I could use the local languages (French, German, Russian, Ukrainian and Portuguese). Added to the above were the normal demands of a hardship post where resources and personnel were always lacking, but challenges never were. My staff and I spent considerable time preparing for a move to a new embassy compound, and helping a company navigate roadblocks and setbacks so it could build us the safe, modern housing we needed. Everyone at the embassy also worked long, hard hours on President George W. Bush's official visit.

Dear Reader, a cautionary note is necessary before comparing Frankfurt with 800 people and two dozen agencies and Embassy Tbilisi with 650 staff and two dozen agencies. In Frankfurt, most employees were senior Americans officers, or foreign service national staff who were experts in financial management, personnel, consular and other fields. Their work had regional and often international components. In Tbilisi, in contrast, only 115 people were Americans, and the majority of the remaining 535 staff were local guards, drivers, mechanics, maintenance personnel, janitorial staff and other service and support personnel. The work of the embassy was focused primarily on Georgia.

My primary responsibilities as management officer at U.S. Embassy Tbilisi were threefold: 1) develop the resources and personnel to make the embassy more productive and effective; 2) support other agencies to enhance their capabilities and through inter-agency coordination increase the embassy's capabilities; and 3) work with the Georgian government and other appropriate parties on legislation and policies that directly affected us. I also worked with the Overseas Building Operations office that was constructing our new embassy facility, and handled logistics for a presidential visit and almost 3000 (no typo!) visitors in one year.

Personnel development was time consuming but paid big dividends. I worked with one new officer on a memo that justified a 50% increase in the embassy's budget after years of growth with no increases that had hamstrung mission operations. Several months later, the officer independently coordinated the reporting for and funding of a $500,000 multi-agency project to support Georgia's national police — a U.S. government priority. My staff was sharp, just inexperienced with State Department policies and procedures. Two remarkable employees had retired from high-level positions in private industry, then joined the State Department after the 9/11 attacks. Another officer, who had worked in real estate for years, successfully concluded a multi-million dollar housing development contract that finally secured safe and modern housing for our American families. The Georgian staff was similarly inexperienced (almost 2/3 hired within the past few years), but dedicated: a number of them, including local guards, volunteered to serve in harm's way at U.S. Embassy, Baghdad.

Supporting other agencies was practically a full-time job. I assisted thousands of temporary visitors, and helped a number of them establish permanent positions as they realized the need for — and cost-effectiveness of — having their own permanent staff on-site. I then helped them navigate the quirks of State Department and Georgian government bureaucracies once they arrived. In one humorous incident, I was called by an agency as the "go-to" person to help establish their presence at the embassy. I talked them through the process and e-mailed them a template cable that they would need to send to the State Department in Washington to justify their request. At the same time, I alerted Washington and the ambassador to the request, and provided the draft approvals each needed to sign off on. All three documents were used almost word-for-word in what was probably the fastest approval for such a request in bureaucratic history.

One agency I helped set up in Tbilisi was the Millennium Challenge Corporation (MCC). MCC provided economic aid to developing countries that had met specific benchmarks for good governance and good economic policies and practices. MCC helped these countries move from relying on foreign assistance to becoming self-sustainable with good government and strong economies. I also worked closely with the Defense Threat Reduction Agency (DTRA), created in 1998 to combat the spread of weapons of mass destruction, with a particular focus on terrorists and rogue states. As nuclear stockpiles had been reduced and remaining weapons were more tightly controlled — think back to Ukraine — terrorists and rogue regimes were now looking for ingredients to make their own weapons of mass destruction. I provided logistical support and guidance to DTRA and helped them expand their presence from intermittent visiting officers to a more permanent presence. This presence helped them in their mission to stop the black market sales of the ingredients needed to make dirty bombs and weapons.

Even dealing with established agencies was time-consuming. The State Department, led by the ambassador, is responsible not only for mission-wide political, economic and assistance policies, but also for oversight to ensure best management practices at all U.S. government agencies in the country. One agency was overpaying for contractual services — and was causing discontent among contractors for the same services with every other U.S. government agency at post. I was asked to review every major contract the agency had — *before* its contracts could be finalized. I also spent many hours with the State Department's Regional Security Officer, responsible for the security of all agencies at post. One agency that was co-located with State Department personnel at a nearby hotel — when the embassy was still spread out throughout Tbilisi — kept insisting that unlike State personnel, "they really didn't need to move" to the more secure new embassy. The agency delayed moving for months until gunfire in the lobby of this hotel shot holes in their argument.

In another case, a U.S. Corps of Engineers employee killed a Georgian in a tragic traffic accident. Thanks to my military connections and Frankfurt experience, I knew that the visitor's "home office" was actually in Turkey, and was able to connect to them and to concerned parties in Washington and at the U.S. European Command. While this was not resolved before I left post, I was confident that the people who needed to be involved were working with the family and the government to ensure a fair resolution to the tragedy,

Legal concerns and taxes consumed an inordinate amount of my time. Nine years after helping develop a mechanism to ensure that local staff paid income taxes in Ukraine, I was doing the same thing in Georgia. My Ukrainian experience was useful, though, as I knew pitfalls to avoid and programs that could work. I met with host government officials, my counterparts from other countries' embassies, non-governmental organizations and some of the U.S. embassy's senior local staff who provided me with reality checks on new procedures that didn't always work as advertised. My deep involvement at all levels gave me the credibility needed to — among other things — convince the other diplomatic missions that they would need to increase their local staff's salaries if they were not currently including a tax component in these payments so their employees could afford to pay taxes. Since this meant significant increases in these embassies annual budgets, this was a hard sell. When the Georgian prime minister who oversaw the development of the fair tax program died (from carbon monoxide poisoning from a faulty space heater) just before it was finalized, everyone involved was saddened, and worried that the program wouldn't be implemented. Thankfully, Georgian lawmakers persevered and enacted the new tax policies and program into law.

It was helpful that there was no ill will on the part of any of the players. Georgian government pronouncements were often ahead of reality, not recognizing that capacity and capabilities in the field weren't keeping up with policy changes. Fortunately, everyone welcomed even negative feedback that helped fix issues. There was no "blame game," bullying or any adverse impact on anyone, from the lowest-level embassy employees to the government bureaucrats, up to and including the Ministers. Rather, everyone worked together to learn from the feedback and used it to fix problems.

In a separate tax issue, I had to justify and defend the tax-free status of almost $200 million in development assistance from the United States. Absent tax-free status, this crucial funding might have been stopped. Shortly afterwards, I had to defend the inviolability of our U.S. diplomatic pouches when someone at the Tbilisi airport suddenly decided these needed to undergo customs inspections. Both situations could have damaged our good relations with — and undermined our ability to provide assistance to — Georgia. I resolved both quickly by providing the Georgians with copies of international law (the Vienna Convention on Diplomatic Relations)[46] and instances in which the Georgians themselves respected and benefitted from the Convention. I was constantly engaged in tracking, reporting on, and working with, frequently changing legislation, policies and processes that could impact the U.S. Embassy.

Supporting the American School in Tbilisi took time too. American Schools are independent organizations, but U.S. missions work closely with them to protect them, the children who attend these schools (children of American embassy employees, children from American businessmen and women and other expatriates), and the many Americans who staff them. Children of Canadians and other close allies also attend these schools. A key example of support is that provided by the embassy's security officer. That officer will periodically review the schools' security, and include the Schools in emergency radio checks and other measures to help ensure American citizen safety.

I even become involved in visa issues. At one point, the embassies of several countries suddenly stopped issuing visas to Georgians, instead requiring them to travel to Moscow where these countries had larger, more established embassies. This almost froze Georgian international travel, because without visas Georgians couldn't go to Frankfurt, for example, which was an interim stop on the way to most other destinations. Fortunately, I was able to work out an agreement with several foreign embassies to continue issuing visas to Georgians locally. Georgian students on U.S.-embassy sponsored academic exchange programs were once again able to travel to their programs in the United States. As the ambassador noted in my annual evaluation, I used my "expertise daily to resolve an array of problems for which there were literally no precedents."

In 2005, the entire embassy moved into high gear for President George W. Bush's official visit to Georgia. On May 10, President Bush spoke at Freedom Square, where massive demonstrations in 2003 led to the resignation of the Georgian government and the installation of a new, pro-Western one. President Bush commended the Georgians, telling them "You gathered here armed with nothing but roses and the power of your convictions and you claimed your liberty. Because you acted, Georgia is today both sovereign and free and a beacon of liberty for this region and the world." (Georgia's revolution inspired the later Orange Revolution in neighboring Ukraine, and others.) President Bush praised

Georgian efforts to fight corruption, reform its economy and to build a democracy where, "the rights of minorities are respected; where a free press flourishes; where a vigorous opposition is welcomed and where unity is achieved through peace,. . . . [and where] the rule of law will prevail and freedom will be the birthright of every citizen".[47] The President later met with embassy personnel and applauded our hard work and success in Georgia which helped achieve that core mission goal to "create a more secure, democratic and prosperous world for the benefit of the American people and the international community." [P13]

This presidential visit was not as grueling as my earlier presidential visits had been thanks to having food, my own bed and a good team that included some of my Frankfurt colleagues. Finding lodging for the hundreds of visitors who participate in, report on and support such a visit was its usual headache, but embassy families hosted some of the visitors so no one shared cots as I had done in Africa. I personally hosted four people in my house, but didn't have the logistics down as well as I'd thought. As I left for the embassy control room before 5 a.m., I was surprised to see one of my Frankfurt specialists sleeping on my living room couch. When he caught up to me hours later, he mentioned that he wasn't sure which room was his when he arrived at 3 a.m., and didn't want to wake anyone up by opening doors and turning on lights to figure it out.

This visit was memorable to me for the "we need two vans for added trips request" that had been slipped under the control room door at some point between midnight (when I left for home) and 5 a.m., when I returned to the control room for the start of another long day. Thanks to my good connection to the head of a major transportation company I managed to obtain the extra vehicles on time. This was a miracle as the company already had all its vehicles in use for the visit, but hey — the company head had almost 2 hours to find two extra vehicles and have them cleaned and ready for duty at the embassy by 8 a.m.!

On a more serious note, the visit was marred by the live grenade that was thrown at Presidents Bush and Saakashvili. It did not go off, and a Georgian security officer hand-carried the grenade far from the crowd. The FBI and Georgian security went through thousands of pictures taken by people at the event to identify the assailant, and Georgian security officers later captured him. Sadly, one agent was killed in the effort.[48]

Gunfire and security concerns were a Tbilisi staple. I recall returning to post after a wonderful family vacation in Ohio, only to discover that both my emergency radio and phone were not working. Jet lagged and exhausted, I heard gunfire all around me, but couldn't get through to the embassy to report in and find out what was going on. After some tense moments recharging my phone, I reached the Marine security guard on duty who reminded me that the Georgians were firing weapons to celebrate a national holiday — it was not the coup or security event I feared. Nevertheless, I slept on the floor that night, on the opposite side of the bed from the windows, to avoid any stray rounds.

The new embassy compound enhanced U.S. Embassy Tbilisi's security and made coordination easier since we were now together in one location. Supporting the construction took up much of my time, though, and was often frustrating. First, there were the security and logistical details involved in moving all U.S. government agencies to the new site. Among other issues, not all agencies had budgeted for the higher costs of the more secure new facility. I also addressed legal issues concerning the many third-country nationals who were working on site, helped with shipments that were held up, and met with a constant stream of inspectors and others who checked on or assisted in various parts of the construction. Fortunately, we had an excellent Overseas Building Operations team on site, and an embassy team that pulled together in an almost seamless move to the new facility in about a week. No essential services were disrupted during this major relocation.

Once finished, this purpose-built "fortress" embassy made us all safer. As with many recently constructed U.S. embassies, however, it was far from the city center and difficult to access.[49] I invited a number of my counterparts from other missions and organizations for a tour. Three arrived late due to traffic difficulties and all had taken some time to get through the layers of security needed just to meet me in the new embassy's "public" areas. The State Department is still working to find a best balance between security and the accessibility for the outreach and openness diplomats need to do their jobs.

Before I comment on my final responsibilities in Georgia, and despite my onerous workload, I would note that I took time to enjoy Georgia's natural beauty, millennia-old culture, impressive architecture and wonderful food — and to get to know the wonderful Georgians themselves. I went skiing, biking and hiking, visited many famous Georgian churches and historical sites and loved attending dance performances and concerts. I could have spent hours just at the Georgian National Museum in Tbilisi, with its amazing gold jewelry and artifacts collection dating back thousands of years. In short, it was a great tour, and I was honored by the Ambassador's comment in my annual review that I had left post with "a legacy of solid accomplishments . . . that will benefit post for years to come." These accomplishments enabled the United States to better support Georgia as it continued on its journey towards becoming a more democratic, prosperous and secure nation.

Back at the office, my final responsibility was to serve as Acting Deputy Chief of Mission (A/DCM), the second highest leadership position in the embassy. The good relations I'd fostered with all agencies as management officer and my comprehensive knowledge of the embassy and country served me well. Embassy Tbilisi had a great team, and it was a pleasure to work with them as we made significant progress in supporting Georgia's move towards good governance and democracy.

As A/DCM, I attended multinational intergovernmental Organization for Security and Cooperation in Europe (OSCE) meetings. The OSCE was created in 1975 for dialogue and negotiation between East and West on security concerns that range from the political and economic to environmental and human concerns (such as refugees and other displaced persons). I've frequently mentioned how U.S. interests are damaged by severe and persistent staffing gaps. Simply put, if we don't attend meetings, we can't influence the issues being addressed at them. If we have "acting" or temporary personnel attending the meetings, we may have less influence for a variety of reasons: an ambassador selected by the president and confirmed by the Senate inherently has more authority than a temporary replacement.

I've mentioned credibility before as an important attribute for diplomacy. As I write this in August 2020, dear reader, I am very concerned that U.S. credibility has been severely damaged by the Trump Administration. Diplomats have to explain life in the United States to foreigners: everything from U.S. government policies and practices to what's happening in the country. When the United States initially supports and defends — then backtrack from and denounces — our allies and our painstakingly crafted and hard-won international agreements that help protect the planet and its people, as well as U.S. programs, policies, and principles, the United States is no longer trusted. When President Trump contradicts himself and facts on the ground, our credibility is damaged. When he undermines and fires government employees who have pledged to uphold the U.S. Constitution that is the very basis of our nation and who valiantly serve our nation through hardships and in danger, our credibility vanishes.

Further, by undermining our own principles, we no longer have the moral authority to call out the bad policies and practices of others. We no longer serve as a model for the world, or a beacon of hope. President Lincoln's second inaugural address beautifully states the ideals of the United States: "With malice toward none, with charity for all . . . [we] may achieve and cherish a just and lasting peace among ourselves and with all nations." Today, we've been at war in Afghanistan since 2001 (almost two decades), yet there is no careful, strategic plan in place for a withdrawal of U.S forces. We defended our allies against Syria's devastating attacks, particularly against civilians, and then pulled out in a unexpected and poorly planned and explained withdrawal that caused countless casualties both among our military allies and innocent civilians. The Trump administration has delayed and threatened to cancel health funding at a time of an international pandemic; separated refugee children from their parents and detained them in appalling conditions; pulled back from agreements to limit and oversee nuclear proliferation; and imposed sanctions and instituted tariffs that may negatively impact other countries but also hurt the United States.

In the past, the United States earned international acclaim, admiration and respect for its efforts to promote peace, help countries rebuild after war (the Marshall Plan mentioned previously), defend freedom and protect the innocent, particularly during the Cold War. I faced bombs and bullets as a diplomat, but I also benefitted from this respect and admiration. People listened to me because they believed that I, as a U.S. government representative, could — and would — help. Our actions speak louder than our words. Today, we ignore and undermine international conventions and practice hypocrisy instead of good governance. As a result our actions are condemned world-wide.

In the United States on June 1, 2020, I was appalled to see security officers gassing unarmed, peaceful protesters exercising their Constitutional rights of free speech and assembly in this nation's capital. Tear gas was banned in 1925 for use in war, in part due to the horrific damage it caused to soldiers during WWI.[50] Yet tear gas and physical force were used in 2020 in Washington D.C. to push innocent civilians back to accommodate a presidential photo shoot.

We can, nevertheless, still hope. We can use this travesty to show leadership to the world. In an American tradition, we can acknowledge our mistakes and learn from them to enact laws, policies and procedures to address persistent racism in the United States. Positive action will honor the memory of George Floyd and others killed by the police, as well as the tens of thousands of peaceful protesters who continued to gather to protest injustice. Positive action can also help protect the vast majority of police officers who honor their oath to protect and serve. By taking action to effect a "more perfect union," we can prove to the world that we are not defined by the actions of the racist few, but that we can come together to make a better world for all.

In my dedication to this book, we recalled the sacrifices the United States made in two world wars — and the Marshall Plan that the U.S. government developed and executed with international partners to help Europe rebuild. I mentioned a Tbilisi colleague who, as thanks for bringing democracy and freedom to his country, volunteered to serve at U.S. Embassy Baghdad. I, and so many others, have worked hard, often in harm's way, to carry out good policies and make some small corners of the world better. In Chapter 15, the conclusion to this book, I call upon everyone — private citizen, media influencer, politician or judge — to speak up and speak out against injustice. Further, to take active measures to return to America's core ideals, and to work at home within our communities — and with our international partners — to achieve peace and justice in this world.

But please join me now on one last assignment, to the State Department's National Foreign Affairs Training Center in Arlington, Virginia.

14

THE FOREIGN SERVICE INSTITUTION (FSI) – GOOD GOVERNMENT ROCKS
ARLINGTON, VIRGINIA, 2006-2009

In 2006, I was honored to be assigned as Associate Dean to the Foreign Service Institute's School of Language Studies. FSI, also known as the National Foreign Affairs Training Center (NFATC), is on the grounds of the facility where Japanese code was broken in WWII, so it is interesting that foreign languages and communication are once again part of the facility's core mission. I had successfully used six languages (French, German, Portuguese, Russian, Ukrainian — and yes, English) in a wide variety of positions during the course of my career. Further, I had extensive experience in training, including in online training. I had also studied at FSI previously, including the 10 months I spent studying Ukrainian. I was excited to be able to share my expertise in order to expand and improve the State Department's language training programs.

Throughout this book, I have noted that words matter. Further, I talked about the great goodwill that I, and therefore the United States, gained when I was in newly independent Ukraine speaking Ukrainian. I emphasized the efficiencies and effectiveness of conducting diplomacy in the host country's language. I've cited démarches and meetings in which I've used my language, professional knowledge and cultural insights to influence other to support U.S. goals. At FSI, I had a chance to provide others with the tools to do the same.

Previously, I described the rigorous exam process applicants must pass to become Foreign Service Officers: the written test of knowledge, a practical exercise that tests negotiation, situational awareness and other skills and abilities, and an interview in which the applicant must demonstrate quick thinking and grace under pressure. I've also detailed the annual "up-or-out" evaluation process which demands that Foreign Service officers note their accomplishments, *and* demonstrate professional expertise and leadership qualities to prove they will be able to perform successfully at ever higher levels of responsibility. A final component of a Foreign Service Officer's professional career is training, and training is what the Foreign Service Institute is all about.

Expertise matters. At FSI, I was able to provide the training that helped my colleagues expand their knowledge and sharpen the skills and abilities they needed to protect America and Americans and successfully carry out U.S. national strategic goals. At FSI, we determined what personnel in the field needed to know and figured out how to get them this knowledge. We made diplomats more effective and efficient so they could successfully implement U.S. government policies and programs and meet U.S. government goals, despite challenges ranging from constant personnel and resource shortages, to foreign government efforts to ignore or avoid inconvenient facts and use propaganda to counter our efforts, and in the face of civil strife, terrorism and war.

At FSI, as overseas, our programs and performance were constantly evaluated. We excelled. In 2006, the State Department received top scores from the Office of Management and Budget in meeting the "President's Management Agenda"[51] goals for best service: strategic use of human capital, competitive sourcing, expanded use of e-government, improved financial performance, and budget and performance integration that ensured we were investing the most money in our highest priorities. That same year, State also received top scores for having the right numbers of people in the right places (rightsizing) to address policy goals, and for property management initiatives, issues I'd worked on throughout my career. In 2007, FSI was designated as one of only five federal-wide e-providers in recognition of the excellence of our programs. Not coincidentally, this avoided the wasteful duplication of these programs by other agencies. It was a pleasure to work at FSI during these exciting times, and to be recognized for our good work.

If my Frankfurt tour was "Roving on Steroids," this tour was even bigger and better, because I had the creative personnel and resources of an entire school to draw upon. Keep in mind that both personnel and resources were limited as the State Department was still playing catch-up from years of budget and personnel cuts. Nevertheless, we made extraordinary progress training thousands of traditional and online students to help them carry out U.S government programs.

We still had resource constraints, but funding and personnel were both increasing to meet the demands of U.S. strategic interests and global leadership. The student body, including part-time and virtual students scattered across the globe, was growing by 14% annually. Our teaching staff, native speakers from over 100 countries, was increasing too. To accommodate training thousands of students with no new space, we scheduled more than 300 classes in shifts in 185 classrooms.

In one unplanned tour of the facilities with the people who controlled our budget, we fortuitously encountered two teachers working on one computer in a crowded little office. They nervously explained that they didn't have their own offices or computers yet, but were "borrowing" a colleague's when she was in class. As we were moving towards online platforms for all our material for 24/7 access to up-to-date authentic language materials, teachers without computers were a problem. By the time I left FSI — after major disruptions as every office was reconfigured to accommodate more instructors and a new annex was built to finally provide urgently needed additional office space — each instructor had a desk and a computer, even if it was occasionally shared in planned shifts. Every student, whether full-time, part-time or "virtual," had access to current, authentic language material — a far cry from the days when I was scouring the town for any material in Ukrainian.

With my years of experience of "doing more with less," I fully exploited our $20 million annual budget and 550-person staff to provide instruction both traditionally and online to almost 5000 students, including from the military, USAID and other government agencies. To accomplish this, I worked closely with the three other FSI Schools, other State Department bureaus and offices, and other agencies and organizations. My supervisor noted in my annual evaluation that potential savings from my distance learning programs were at least $1 million. I looked at it as, "This was money we didn't have, and an urgent need that I nevertheless met."

To explain a bit about my job as Associate Dean at FSI's School of Language Studies, a quick overview of its components is in order.

First: language training. This is time intensive and can be difficult. After all, you can't just plug brains in for instant knowledge transfers. Yet foreign language competency is crucial to diplomacy, and the State Department recognizes this. Diplomats cannot be tenured, let alone be promoted to senior levels, unless they have good language skills and the cultural knowledge that comes along with them. The State Department has neither the funding nor personnel needed to train everyone in the necessary languages. So, whenever possible, it hires new diplomats who already possess language skills — all other qualifications being equal — over those who have none, particularly in difficult-to-learn languages in high demand such as Chinese and Arabic.

Of course, the State Department must be flexible to meet changing U.S. government priorities. After the fall of the Soviet Union in 1991, for example, there was a surge in Russian language training and in national languages such as Ukrainian. Later, as Embassies Baghdad and Kabul grew, we expanded our Arabic, Pashto, and Dari training programs. Conversely, when we closed our embassy in Iran, we reduced Farsi training. Many of the 550 staff I supported were contractors, which meant they could be hired quickly — or their contracts not renewed — depending upon these constantly changing needs.

The U.S. government benefited from the flexiblility of using contractors to provide targeted training, while avoiding the expense of hiring full-time instructors. That said, I firmly believe that we need to take better care of contractors and specifically, ensure a nation-wide health insurance program that is not linked to an individual company or job.

In my experiences with federal government, unpredictable shutdowns — whether for snowstorms or politicking about the federal budget — severely harmed our contractors. Regular employees received back pay, but contractors did not. This was particularly painful for them during the government shutdown from December 22, 2018 until January 25, 2019, which was the longest shutdown ever and the second shutdown of the Trump administration. It is hard to attract and retain the best people for any job with no guarantees of work or salary, and it's unfair to ask contractors to bear the burden of job insecurity despite holding contracts.

Contractor issues were of concern to me throughout my career. Although contractors were responsible for purchasing their own life and health insurance, they often had to pay expensive individual rates they could not afford. For this reason and others, they often did not purchase insurance. In 1998 at the U.S. embassies in Nairobi, Kenya and Dar es Salaam, Tanzania, many contractors who had served the U.S. government for years had no insurance benefits. This became tragic as so many were killed or injured in the bombings there. I was proud to be one of the many U.S. citizens who donated money to help pay for their medical treatments, but these long-term employees should not have had to worry about paying for treatment for injuries occurred in the line of duty. Freedom from want, freedom from fear and a certain stability in life are crucial to "life, liberty and the pursuit of happiness" enshrined in our Declaration of Independence.

The rise of the contractor and "temp" worker economy worries me. I have seen contractors struggling to find the next contract to support their families. The constant fear of not getting that next job, of losing a job, of not getting paid on time — or at all — and the overwhelming fear of not being able to take care of family in the face of a catastrophic illness or accident are fears that no human being should suffer. Security is not just a concern about bombs and bullets. Security is also freedom from worry about health care, life insurance, and even the basic worry about being able to feed and take care of one's self and one's family. The United States has acquired the reputation of putting monetary gain over human welfare, and particularly, of seeking short-term profits at the expense of workers. As a nation, we can do better. At FSI, I was proud to be able to regularize the status of dozens of contractors who had worked for decades for the State Department.

Getting the right instructors at the right time was just one aspect of my job. We also had to ensure that we had the right students, to ensure we had the right people with the language they needed in the field. To meet this goal, I participated in "language-designated position" reviews. Human resource officers, subject matter experts such as political, consular or security officers, representatives from posts and I (as the language and training expert) met to determine which positions at a given post needed what level of language expertise. Many decisions were clear-cut. But then — should we cut a Chinese- language-designated position in Vancouver Canada that was valuable in dealing with the large Chinese-speaking population there? And if we skimped on language training and sent someone out at a lower level of competency — would that lead to serious trouble? What were our priorities, as we never could cover all language training needed?

Answering these questions was difficult. The Foreign Service uses a "language proficiency scale" of one to five, with "one" being a bare minimum that would give a student a "life skills" vocabulary to get around town and to offer basic courtesies in the host country. "Five" is college-educated native speaker level, with "three" being general professional proficiency. General professional proficiency is by no means perfect, but it is what enabled me to prevent a generator breakdown when I called out "demobilize" the generator instead of "turn it off." At professional proficiency level I could make myself understood, and through continual learning, improve and expand the professional vocabulary I needed to perform well in a given job. For more nuanced negotiations, diplomats must obtain at least a "4" level, and may also call upon professional translators (of written texts) and interpreters (of the spoken word).

Hiring diplomats who already had language skills and putting them to work in language-designated positions was extremely cost-effective. The School of Language Studies also cut language training costs by exploiting language skills that could be applied to other, similar, languages. For example, one officer with strong Spanish skills tested at "professional-level competency" in Portuguese after taking online *"Spanish to Portuguese Conversion"* classes. He used his knowledge of these similar languages in part-time virtual training to obtain results that would have taken a typical student six months of classroom study. The cost to develop the course was about $35,000. Room and board for just a single government employee in Washington D.C. in 2008 was $109/day, which, with travel, would have cost the US Government about $20,000 per student to achieve the same result. All our Distance Learning courses quickly paid for themselves by providing convenient, urgently needed training to thousands.

Distance Learning also provided timely, focused training. Our "Out and About" online language series for posts from Moscow to Beijing helped thousands of people:

everyone from the spouses of U.S. government personnel assigned to Moscow, to U.S. government employees and others in Beijing, including those who provided assistance at the 2008 Beijing Olympics. Moscow "Out and About" had the added benefit of meeting a Congressional mandate: a Congressional delegation visiting Moscow realized that diplomatic spouses were virtual prisoners at the embassy if they couldn't read signs in Cyrillic and had no Russian language that would enable them to leave the embassy compound for groceries, medical appointments or other basics of life. Congress said "fix this" — and we did.

We also developed Consular and Public Diplomacy courses, focusing on new priorities and guidance (think back to the Diversity Visa and other new programs I dealt with in Montreal) and rapidly produced Compact Discs in a variety of languages for hundreds of officers. Distance Learning — everything from stand-alone CDs for posts with poor Internet connectivity, to instructor-supported online learning — did not replace classroom learning, but significantly augmented the quantity of training we provided to people. It also provided training to employees who otherwise might have received none. Not coincidentally, many of the spouses who took language training used their new language skills to fill — and successfully perform in — positions at posts which might otherwise have gone vacant, directly benefitting and strengthening U.S. embassies worldwide.

The School of Language Studies also had field schools in Tunis, Yokohama, Seoul and Taipei, to provide a second year of intensive Arabic, Japanese, Korean and Chinese studies, respectively. Students often took two years or more to acquire professional proficiency in these difficult languages, and the field schools helped them attain that proficiency through guided immersion study. The School of

Language Studies also provided funding for local-hire language instructors at most posts to help officers and spouses maintain and improve their language skills. This included providing timely, targeted support (specific vocabulary, for example) for country-specific issues.

A second component of my job was coordinating with the other professional schools at FSI: the School of Applied Information Technology (SAIT), the School of Professional and Area Studies (SPAS), and the Leadership and Management School (LMS). As Associate Dean I worked closely with them to determine: what do diplomats need to know: what do they need to do; and,what are the tools required to meet these needs? And specifically, how can FSI provide them what they need as efficiently and effectively as possible so they, in turn, can go out into the world and safeguard U.S. interests.

The School of Applied Information Technology (SAIT) was particularly important to me. I loved working with its talented, creative experts to develop new training techniques and instructional products. I was especially proud of overseeing the installation of the School of Language Studies first electronic blackboards, and even more proud that we had over 150 installed within 3 years, with over 300 instructors trained on their use by 2009. We used the latest technology available, while always looking for even newer and better ideas and technology. In one instance, an officer — who already spoke fluent Spanish — wanted to learn the indigenous Guarani language while he waited for his Senate hearing confirming his nomination as Ambassador to Paraguay. We couldn't find a Guarani instructor in Washington, but SAIT was able to connect him virtually with an instructor in Paraguay. The 90 percent of Paraguayans who speak Guarani greatly appreciated his efforts.

The Leadership and Management School (LMS) did well delivering leadership training to everyone who needed it, ranging from the newest employees (I supervised 72 people as a first-tour officer in Africa) up to ambassadors. LMS also delivered essential crisis management training to people and posts. When I worked in the Bureau of Diplomatic Security, I participated in a crisis management exercise at one coup-prone post. These exercises were carefully tailored to each post's potential problems — and for real life chaos, the Washington team had a hidden microphone in the room where all key officers at the post were handling the constructed crisis. In my exercise, we overheard the ambassador correctly note "We'll have to call the "Number 2 in the Defense Ministry." We were ready, as "the Defense Ministry" to report that the "Number 2" had been killed so we could see how deep their country knowledge ran, and if they knew who the "Number 3" and even "4" were. Remember Burundi when I did *not* have the keys to my motor pool in case we had to evacuate post? Or Mali where one intrepid officer took a dugout canoe to get to the embassy when a local bridge was flooded?[P5] These exercises provided written records for embassies of as much information as possible, so that when crises arose, they had essential details at their fingertips, even if post personnel had changed.[P5]

Security and preparing for crises were central to FSI's mission. The School of Language Studies joined with LMS to develop, among other products, the CD course with key Arabic terms for employees heading to Embassy Baghdad. This "Out and About" Baghdad had a huge security component ("don't shoot," "it's a bomb") and expressions and terminology not needed at your standard posts.

The School of Professional and Areas Studies (SPAS) covered everything from orientation through political, consular, management, public diplomacy — and even general services studies. The School of Language Studies instructors worked closely with SPAS on all subjects, and I know employees appreciated the local-language lists of contracting, leasing, maintenance, motor vehicle and other vocabulary that would have been so helpful to me in Ukraine. Foreign Service personnel also appreciated terminology on newer issues such as climate change, emerging diseases, etc. The School of Language Studies created a number of CDs to help posts roll-out new policies and programs, and worked to develop authentic training in public diplomacy (hard enough to do public speaking in your own language, let alone a foreign one) and other country-specific training. For example, students going to Afghanistan participated in simulated "loya jirgas," the meetings of Afghan elders who were instrumental to governance in the country. Bottom line, we had authentic language materials on everything from economic and consular affairs, to budget and contracting, medicine and information technology — and including on issues such as terrorism, food security, democracy and human rights.

The School of Language Studies also worked with other agencies, academia, the military and others to identify best practices and new tools — anything that could help us be more productive. When we developed an excellent new online course, we shared the template across languages so the courses could be quickly duplicated with the appropriate tweaks to reflect cultural and linguistic differences as needed. Our expertise in training and testing was recognized nation-wide, and students could receive credit at academic institutions based on their SLS language test scores. In short, we worked with the experts we needed across many disciplines to prepare students to succeed. We gave diplomats the tools they required to work towards that "more secure, democratic and prosperous world for the benefit of the American people and the international community."

I was honored to serve America for 25 years. My career was demanding, but also stimulating and rewarding. In 2009 I retired from the Foreign Service, but did not "retire" from trying to make the world a better place. I've been a teacher, helping to prepare the next generation of activists and advocates, and have volunteered with a number of charitable organizations.

I have also stayed involved with the foreign affairs community and foreign affairs. I've volunteered with the Associates of the American Foreign Service Worldwide (AAFSW), which focuses on supporting family members in the diplomatic community, and support the American Foreign Service Association, the professional organization/ union of America's diplomats. I have done public speaking, written editorials and visited the halls of Congress to lobby on foreign affairs issues. I have tried to use my expertise and experiences to continue to have a positive impact on the planet we share.

As I end this book, I'd like to thank you for sharing my journey with me. I hope I've convinced you that democracy and diplomacy can make a difference in this world, and that both are worth nurturing and defending.

Please join me now in my final chapter, a call to action: I ask that you, dear readers, use *your* knowledge, skills and abilities to support and defend democracy, diplomacy and the diplomats and public servants who are on the front lines in these troubling times.

15

A CALL TO ACTION

Dear readers, I have given numerous examples of how the power of ideals — given patience and persistence in their pursuit — can make a difference in the world. I hope I've persuaded you that freedom, democracy and good governance — truth, justice, accountability and equal treatment and opportunity for all — matter, and that having professionals who can advocate for these ideals and work to implement them can lead to a more peaceful, prosperous and secure world. Finally, I hope that I've convinced you that it is in the U.S. national interest for us to be engaged in the world — and that investing in the diplomats who are the front line defense for the United States will lead to a more prosperous and secure world for all.

I promised "no tests," and will honor that promise. But I challenge you to help advocate for and sustain the tenets of American democracy at this critical time when they are being seriously threatened. I challenge you to honor the service and sacrifice of America's diplomats and others who continue to work towards our more perfect union and a better world. Help us return to a time when America was respected for the creativity and "can-do" attitude that won two world wars and a cold war, sent men to the moon, conquered polio and brought a time of peace to the planet. The United States is not perfect, but we all can help it take steps "towards that more perfect union." Help stop the hypocrisy that calls for democracy and good governance abroad while we undermine our own at home. Help the United States regain its global leadership which, at its best, worked towards peace and was esteemed for its compassion towards all, a model for the world.

So, whether you are president or politician, private person, media influencer or mogul, or a judge, I ask that you do what you can to honor the service and sacrifice of those who have gone into harm's way to protect and serve the United States. This, then, is my challenge to you:

I. AS A PRIVATE CITIZEN:

I mentioned Rosa Parks previously, as one woman who ignited a movement by one small action: she demanded dignity and respect and refused to move to the back of the bus. A government "of the people, by the people and for the people" is only as good as we are, and as we demand it to be. The following are suggestions for small steps that we can all take.

Be a thoughtful, informed citizen and VOTE!

I've served in countries where voters have stood in line long hours under a burning sun, or faced bullying, beatings and even death to vote. In 2000, George W. Bush won the presidential election over Al Gore by only 537 votes out of about 6 million cast in Florida. Other votes, including in local elections, have been this close and the results have impacted our lives.

Stay informed.

Both traditional — and certainly social — media have lost credibility in the rush to publish and the push to offer opinion and spin as fact. Demand facts over opinion and hold traditional media and today's Internet influencers accountable — for playing fast and loose with the truth, presenting rumor and opinion as fact, for uncivil discourse, and for inciting hatred and division.

Demand truth, accountability, and action from politicians.

Hold politicians to the same standards to which we are held. At a minimum, make politicians "show us the money." Are they being funded by Chevron or Greenpeace, labor unions or big business? Are they serving their constituents and the long-term interest of this country — or are they serving themselves and special interests?

Don't settle for politics as usual, but demand that politicians act to address today's issues and make the world better for us all. Vote them out of office if they are not doing their jobs.

As a diplomat, I had to file financial disclosure forms: proof that I was not profiting from my work. I could be fired for making disparaging remarks about people based on their race, sex, color, religion, disability, national origin, or age. If I lied, I would lose my security clearance and my job. Incompetence, either not knowing the rules of my job or not performing it successfully, would again be grounds for dismissal. Pandering to a lobbyist or interest group would have led to a closer review of my financial disclosures and could be grounds for dismissal. Failing miserably at most of the job while — perhaps — making headway on one "special interest" would lead to my separation from the Foreign Service.

If we permit low expectations for our elected officials, some officials will lower themselves to meet them.

Speak up and speak out.

Take up a cause toward good governance: truth, justice, accountability and equal treatment and opportunity for all. Don't support short-term, self-centered enrichment. Advocate instead for long-term policies and practices that will strengthen the United States and ensure a better future for our children and our children's children. Write letters to the editor, to a senator or representative or even the president: together we will be heard. We must speak out against despotism, injustice, and a government of the elite and for the elite.

Support diplomats, scientists, medical professionals, teachers and other experts who usually toil far from the spotlight.

They work daily to make a positive difference in our lives — whether for clean air and water, product safety, peace, preparing the next generation of citizens and other good causes. Today, experts are in the spotlight risking their lives to save ours in this coronavirus pandemic. In 2020, many have lost their lives due to a lack of basic personal protection equipment such as gowns and gloves. Do not denigrate them. Honor their expertise and sacrifices. Do not forget them as we move beyond the current crisis. After this crisis, fund them so they will be better prepared to handle the next one that will surely come.

II. FOR THE TRADITIONAL AND NON-TRADITIONAL MEDIA, INCLUDING ONLINE INFLUENCERS:

Give us the facts.

Tell us the truth, the whole truth and nothing but the truth. Leave the pontificating and opinions at home — or clearly label them as such. Do not incite hatred, support demagoguery, and disseminate propaganda.

Don't hide ugliness behind anonymity.

Tell us who you are and where your money is coming from, particularly if it is coming from foreign sources, and we'll decide how "accurate" your "news" is.

Attack policies, not people, and speak civilly at all times.

III. FOR THE POLITICIAN — AT EVERY LEVEL:

Act with honor and integrity, and fulfill your sworn duty.

Don't kick the can down the road on the critical issues of the day such as income inequality, homelessness, climate change, a new revolution of twenty-first century industry and technology, endless wars and the hunger in America, particularly among our children and the elderly, that is a national disgrace. People deserve security — from hunger, homelessness, joblessness, lack of healthcare and other worries. Provide people equal opportunities in the pursuit of happiness. Problems ignored or deferred don't go away — they just grow into bigger and more complex problems that become even more difficult to solve.

Don't live in the past.

Explore and exploit the potential of the present and future. Industries rise and fall: photographs and phone operators are out, digital imaging and computer programmers are in, and fossil fuels are being rapidly replaced by renewable energies. The pace of change is staggering, but Americans have adapted before. Most importantly, there are good jobs — and money to be made — if we educate the workforce to work in and exploit new technologies, including in renewable energy. Fighting against change will only beggar us all.

So:

• At the federal level, address the bigger challenges that local authorities cannot. Lack of federal leadership and guidance on Covid-19, for example, has led us to chaos and needless, tragic deaths. First responders and medical professionals have died for lack of personal protection equipment, state governors are competing with one another (and driving prices up) for these limited resources, and a patchwork of mask and travel restrictions have left gaping holes in this country's defenses against Covid-19. As a result, the United States has one of the highest per capita death rates of almost any country on the planet.

- Honor the experts. Scientists, engineers and others got us to the moon and back, and the research and development for our space programs gave us innovations and prosperity. Fund and help foster better education in math, English, science, civics, history and even the fundamentals of diplomacy, or "how to get along in a complex and constantly changing world." Fund and support the experts and their research and development that will help us prosper and make us world leaders again.

- Be honest. Don't be afraid to admit a mistake, or to change your ideas as you learn more or as unexpected consequences may require. Think of how African Americans and women finally secured the right to vote. Neither was easy or quick and more work remains to be done, but Ignoring today's critical tough issues will not solve them, but will lead to bigger and more challenging problems.

- Above all, respect and obey the law and provide equal justice for all. Don't make politics about ego, power or money, but about the protecting the least of your constituents and protecting the future for us all. When our laws are not just, or when they give the electorate the proverbial "bread and circuses" in the short term vs. the long term better good for all — change the laws to strive for that "more perfect union."

IV. FOR THE JUDICIARY:

Do your sworn duty.

Fulfill your responsibilities as the independent third branch of government, protecting the Constitution and the people it serves. Do not politicize your work, but do weigh in on issues such as gerrymandering and other actions that have taken away so many people's rights and abilities to vote.

Don't delay.

Promptly address those issues that daily impact American lives in a fair, just way. In just one example, the 1954 decision in Brown v. Board of Education of Topeka determined that racial discrimination and segregated schools based on race were illegal. Today, the Supreme Court seems to support segregation based on wealth — local property taxes paying for widely unequal school systems that do not provide equal opportunity to the poor. Use the law as a force for positive change, and not as chains to oppress.

Do not cater to money and those who have it.

When a corporation counts for more than an individual, when individual rights are trampled upon — our incarceration rates disproportionately impact people of color and the poor — "equal treatment under the law" becomes a mockery and our democracy is weakened.

Empires fall. Think of the Roman empire, the Ottoman Empire, the Russian Empire and the British Empire. Recently I saw a copy of a document written in French around 1880 from the head of the 500-year-old Ottoman empire to the

Czar of Russia. Two of the most powerful empires of the day, using a language foreign to both to communicate. Today neither empire exists, and English is our global language. Who knows where the United States is headed? Certainly, together we stand, divided we will fall, and wasted resources and short-sighted policies that undermine the foundations of our democracy and democratic institutions will accelerate the fall.

We have an amazing nation that is rich in human capital and natural resources, but we can't afford to squander them forever. Truth should also not be squandered, but should be used to identify and address the problems that are leading to our decline. Dear reader, join with me to support those ideals that will strengthen our country and put us once more on a path towards that "more perfect union." Nurture the Untied States of America that I and other diplomats, the military and other public servants are working to strengthen, protect and help prosper.

In honor and in memory of Michelle Deney, Bill Bultemeier and the many unsung diplomats who have died for their country, I offer this quotation. These last sentences from the Gettysburg address were written for the Civil War dead, but hold true for all who have given their lives for the United States.

It is for us the living ... that we here highly resolve that these dead shall not have died in vain—that this nation, under God, shall have a new birth of freedom—and that government of the people, by the people, for the people, shall not perish from the earth.

—ABRAHAM LINCOLN

ACKNOWLEDGEMENT

I am grateful to Margaret Caton, Rose Esber and Susan Nelson for their inspiration, guidance, superb editing and constant encouragement.

I am also grateful to Scott and Melissa Stricker who provided thoughtful insights that inspired me to reach out to a broader audience beyond the foreign affairs community and to Victoria Silverman, whose editing provided both keen insights and polish to the finished product. Other editors who made this book better include Ruth Ann Skaff and Karen Krueger.

I would also like to thank graphic designer Lolan O'Rourke of O.Designs, who digitized, restored and helped lay out the decades-old photographs that aid in telling this story, Alan Hebel of theBookDesigners who prepped the book so beautifully for publication and Indexing Research for their indexing expertise.

ENDNOTES

1. U.S. Department of Justice, Office of Public Affairs, "Malian National Sentenced to 25 Years in Prison for Conspiracy to Murder U.S. Diplomat," Press Release, April 26, 2016, https://www.justice.gov/opa/pr/malian-national-sentenced-25-years-prison-conspiracy-murder-us-diplomat.

2. Atomic Archive, "US-Russia-Ukraine Trilateral Statement and Annex," accessed July 1, 2020, http://www.atomicarchive.com/Docs/Deterrence/Trilateral.shtml.

3. U.S. Department of State, Bureau of Public Affairs, "Ukraine Relations," Fact Sheet, June 18, 1997, https://1997-2001.state.gov/regions/nis/fs-us_ukr_970618.html.

4. Thomas H., Armstrong, "Withholding of Ukraine Security Assistance," U.S. Government Accountability Office Decision File B-331564, released January 16, 2020, https://www.gao.gov/assets/710/703909.pdf.

5. U.S. Department of State, "U.S. Embassy Berlin, Backgrounder on the Pendleton Act," U.S. Embassy Berlin Backgrounder, accessed July 1, 2020 https://usa.usembassy.de/etexts/democrac/28.htm.

6. U.S. Office of Special Counsel, "Hatch Overview," OSC website definition, accessed July 1, 2020, https://osc.gov/Services/Pages/HatchAct.aspx.

7. Jack Maskell, "Financial Disclosure by Federal Officials and Publication of Disclosure Reports," Congressional Research Service Report R43186, released August 22, 2013, https://fas.org/sgp/crs/misc/R43186.pdf.

8. U.S. Department of State Office of the Historian, "The Rogers Act," accessed July 1, 2020, https://history.state.gov/departmenthistory/short-history/rogers.

9. Association for Diplomatic Studies & Training, "The Foreign Service Exam – Finding a More Diverse FSO," accessed July 1, 2020, https://adst.org/2016/08/foreign-service-exam-finding-diverse-fso/.

10. Dan Manga, "Trump's Cabinet has been rocked by a number of ethics scandals — here's a complete guide," CNBC, updated February 16, 2018, https://www.cnbccom/2018/02/15/trump-cabinet-officials-in-ethics-scandals.html.

11. Alina Selyuk and Lucia Maffei, "Who Oversees The President's Ethics? Here's Our List," National Pubic Radio, March 27, 2017, https://www.npr.org/2017/03/27/520983699/who-oversees-the-president-s-ethics-a-reference-sheet.

12 Cornell Law School Legal Information Institute 5 U.S. Code § 3331, Cornell Law School, Oath of office, accessed July 1, 2020, https://www.law.cornell.edu/uscode/text/5/3331.

13. Harry Kopp, "Speaking Out," The Foreign Service Journal, American Foreign Service Association, January/February 2020, https://www.afsa.org/truth-and-honor.
*For further information On John Paton Davies' story: https://en.wikipediaorg/wiki/John_Paton_Davies_Jr

14. Jeffrey R. Smith, "Timeline: How Trump Withheld Ukraine Aid," the Center for Public Integrity #UKRAINEDOCS, December 13, 2019, https://publicintegrity.org/national-security/timeline-how-trump-withheld-ukraine-aid/.

15: U.S. Department of State, The Foreign Affairs Manual for the U.S. Department of State 2 FAM 070, Dissent Channel, CT:GEN-524, September 11, 2018,https://fam.state.gov/fam/02fam/02fam0070.html.

16. Christopher Woolf, "Public Radio International, An ex-ambassador explains the 'dissent channel' that US diplomats are using to protest Trump's travel ban," The World, January 31, 2014, https://www.pri.org/stories/2017-01-31/ex-ambassador-explains-dissent-channel-us-diplomats-are-using-protest-trumps.

17. John Kerry, Remarks at the Chicago Council on Global Affairs, U.S. Department of State Archived Content, October 26, 2016, https://2009-2017.state.gov/secretary/remarks/2016/10/263653.htm.

*The Politifact Website, which checks facts, provides insights that people believe that almost one-third of U.S. government spending goes to Foreign Affairs: https://www.politifact.com/factchecks/2016/nov/09/john-kerry/yep-most-people-clueless-us-foreign-aid-spending/.

18. U.S. Department of State, "Facts About our Most Valuable Asset - Our People," Bureau of Human Resources Fact Sheet, March 31, 2019, https://www.state.gov/wp-content/uploads/2019/05/HR_Factsheet0319.pdf.

19. U.S. Department of Defense, Defense Manpower Data Center (DMDC), DoD Personnel, Workforce Reports & Publications, accessed July 1, 2020, https://www.dmdc.osd.mil/appj/dwp/dwp_reports.jsp.

20. U.S. Department of Defense, National Defense Budget Estimates for FY 20201, April 2020, https://comptroller.defense.gov/Portals/45/Documents/defbudget/fy2021/FY21_Green_Book.pdf.

21. The Economic Times, "China overtakes US in number of diplomatic missions," November 27, 2019, https://economictimes.indiatimes.com/news/international/world-news/china-overtakes-us-in-number-of-diplomatic-missions-study/articleshow/72258473.cms?utm_source=contentofinterest&utm_medium=text&utm_campaign=cppst.

22. U.S. Government Spending, US Federal Budget Overview, accessed July 1, 2020, https://www.usgovernmentspending.com/federal_budget,

23. Craig Whitlock and Bob Woodward, "Pentagon buries evidence of $125 billion in bureaucratic waste." *Washington Post*, December 5, 2016, https://www.washingtonpost.com/investigations/pentagon-buries-evidence-of-125-billion-in-bureaucratic-waste/2016/12/05/e0668c76-9af6-11e6-a0ed-ab0774c1eaa5_story.htm.

24. Joe Gould, "Military brass defend State Department against White House budget ax," Defense News, October 30, 2018, https://www.defensenews.com/digital-show-dailies/sofic/2017/05/09/military-brass-defend-state-department-against-white-house-budget-ax/.

25. CNN, "Gulf War Fast Facts," CNN Library, July 30, 2019 https://www.cnn.com/2013/09/15/world/meast/gulf-war-fast-facts/index.html.

26. Stephen Daggett, "Costs of Major U.S. Wars," Congressional Research Service, June 29, 2010, https://fas.org/sgp/crs/natsec/RS22926.pdf.

*The cost of the Second Gulf War is contested. Some estimates are for the costs of military operations only and do not reflect costs of veterans' benefits, interest on war-related debt, or assistance to allies. Estimates range from $800+ billion to over $1 trillion. Another reputable site about war costs is Brown University's https://watson.brown.edu/costsofwar/.

27. Palmer v. Shultz, 815 F.2d 84 (D.C. Cir. 1987), https://law.justia.com/cases/federal/appellate-courts/F2/815/84/22782/.

28. U.S. Department of State, Bureau of Consular Affairs, "Diversity Visa Program - Entry," 2020, https://travel.state.gov/content/travel/en/us-visas/immigrate/diversity-visa-program-entry.html.

29. U.S. Department of State, Bureau of Consular Affairs, "Visa Waiver" Program, 2020, https://travel.state.gov/content/travel/en/us-visas/tourism-visit/visa-waiver-program.html.

30. Tabitha Marshall, "Oka Crisis," *The Canadian Encyclopedia,* July 11, 2016, https://www.thecanadianencyclopedia.ca/en/article/oka-crisis.

31. John Kerry, Remarks at the Chicago Council on Global Affairs, U.S, Department of State Archived Content, October 26, 2016, https://2009-2017.state.gov/secretary/remarks/2016/10/263653.htm.

32. Nuclear Regulatory Commission, "U.S. Backgrounder on Chernobyl Nuclear Power Plant Accident," Nuclear Regulatory Commission Backgrounder, last updated August 15, 2018, https://www.nrc.gov/reading-rm/doc-collections/fact-sheets/chernobyl-bg.html

33. Library of Congress, "Ukraine Famine," Revelations from the Russian Archives, accessed July 1, 2020, https://www.loc.gov/exhibits/archives/ukra.html

34. Bruce W. Nelan, "Bear Hugs All Around." Time, January 24,1994, pp. 38-41.

35. United Nations, "110 Governments Adopt Ambitious Global Programme to Tackle Marine Degradation," Meetings Coverage and Press Releases, Press Release HE/915, November 8, 1995, https://www.un.org/press/en/1995/19951108.he915.html.

36. Spiro, Peter J., "U.S. Supreme Court Knocks Down State Burma Law," American Society of International Law, June 3, 2000, https://www.asil.org/insights/volume/5/issue/7/us-supreme-court-knocks-down-state-burma-law.

37. Vastly Markus and Ihor Stebelsky, "History of Ukraine," The Internet Encyclopedia of Ukraine, accessed July 1, 2020, http://www.encyclopediaofukraine.com/display.asp?linkpath=pages%5CH%5CI%5CHistoryofUkraine.htm.

38. Kofi Annan, Address by Kofi Annan to the Annual Assembly of Heads of State and Government of the Organization of African Unity (OAU), United Nations Secretary - General, June 2, 1997, https://www.un.org/sg/en/content/sg/speeches/1997-06-02/address-kofi-annan-annual-assembly-heads-state-and-government

39. Glen J. Guimond, AFSA website "Examining State's Foreign Service Officer Hiring Today," American Foreign Service Association, accessed July 1, 2020 https://www.afsa.org/examining-states-foreign-service-officer-hiring-today.

40. Stephanie Savell, "America at War, " *Smithsonian,* January 2019, https://www.smithsonianmag.com/history/map-shows-places-world-where-us-military-operates-180970997/.

41. Rukmini Callimachi, Helene Cooper, Eric Schmitt, Alan Blinder and Thomas Gibbons-Neff, "An Endless War': Why 4 U.S. Soldiers Died in a Remote African Desert," *The New York Times,* February 20, 2018, https://www.nytimes.com/interactive/2018/02/17/world/africa/niger-ambush-american-soldiers.html.

42. Roey Hadar and Gewen Ifill Fellow, "Key U.S. Ambassador Posts Remain Vacant," DISQUS. PBS, April 4, 2019, https://www.pbs.org/weta/washingtonweek/blog-post/key-us-ambassador-posts-remain-vacant.

43. U.S. Department of Justice, Office of Public Affairs, "Malian National Sentenced to 25 Years in Prison for Conspiracy to Murder U.S. Diplomat," Press Release, April 26, 2016, April 26, https://www.justice.gov/opa/pr/malian-national-sentenced-25-years-prison-conspiracy-murder-us-diplomat.

* This article also references a 2018 Government Accounting Office (GAO) report that notes that 1 in 7 of Foreign Service Officer positions were vacant at the time.

44. Shane Harris, "Powell's Army," *Government Executive*, November 1, 2003,, https://www.govexec.com/magazine/2003/11/powells-army/15328/.

45. John Brummet et al., "OVERSEAS PRESENCE Framework for Assessing Embassy Staff Levels Can Support Rightsizing Initiatives," Government Accounting Office Report 02-780, p.3, July 2002, https://www.gao.gov/assets/240/235255.pdf.

46. Vienna Convention on Diplomatic Relations, Vienna, 18 April, 1961, United Nations Treaty Series, vol.330, No. 4739, p. 3, https://legal.un.org/ilc/texts/instruments/english/conventions/9_1_1961.pdf.

47. Dana Bash, John King and Jill Dougherty, "Bush: Georgia Beacon of Liberty," CNN, May 10, 2005, http://www.cnn.com/2005/WORLD/europe/05/10/bush.tuesday/.

48. Ryan Chilcote, "Bush Grenade Attacker Gets Life," CNN, January 11, 2006, http://www.cnn.com/2006/WORLD/europe/01/11/georgia.grenade/.

49. Alex Tiersky and Susan Epstein, "Securing U.S. Diplomatic Facilities and Personnel Abroad: Background and Policy Issues," Government Accounting Office Report 7-5700, July 30, 2014, https://fas.org/sgp/crs/row/R42834.pdf.

50. Anna Feigenbaum, "100 Years of Tear Gas A chemical weapon drifts off the battlefield and into the streets," *The Atlantic*, August 16, 2014, https://www.theatlantic.com/ international/archive/2014/08/100-years-of-tear-gas/378632/

51. Congressional Research Service, "The President's Management Agenda: A Brief Introduction," updated January 7, 2009, https://www.everycrsreport.com/reports/RS21416.html.

BIBLIOGRAPHY

Annan, Kofi, Address by Kofi Annan to the Annual Assembly of Heads of State and Government of the Organization of African Unity (OAU), United Nations Secretary - General, June 2, 1997, https://www.un.org/sg/en/content/sg/speeches/1997-06-02/ address-kofi-annan-annual-assembly-heads-state-and-government.

Armstrong, Thomas H., "Withholding of Ukraine Security Assistance," U.S. Government Accountability Office Decision File B-331564, released January 16, 2020, https://www.gao.gov/ assets/710/703909.pdf.

Association for Diplomatic Studies & Training, "The Foreign Service Exam – Finding a More Diverse FSO," accessed July 1, 2020, https://adst.org/2016/08/ foreign-service-exam-finding-diverse-fso/.

Atomic Archive, "US-Russia-Ukraine Trilateral Statement and Annex," accessed July 1, 2020, http://www.atomicarchive.com/ Docs/Deterrence/Trilateral.shtml.

Bash, Dana, John King and Jill Dougherty, "Bush: Georgia Beacon of Liberty," CNN, May 10, 2005, http://www.cnn. com/2005/WORLD/europe/05/10/bush.tuesday/.

Brummet, John, Janey Cohen, Chris Hall, Katie Hartsburg, Lynn Moore and Melissa Pickworth.,"OVERSEAS PRESENCE Framework for Assessing Embassy Staff Levels Can Support Rightsizing Initiatives," Government Accounting Office Report 02-780, p.3, July 2002, https://www.gao.gov/assets/240/235255.pdf.

Callimachi, Rukmini, Helene Cooper, Eric Schmitt, Alan Blinder and Thomas Gibbons-Neff, ""An Endless War': Why 4 U.S. Soldiers Died in a Remote African Desert," The New York Times, February 20, 2018, https://www.nytimes.com/interactive/2018/02/17/world/africa/niger-ambush-american-soldiers.html.

Chilcote, Ryan, "Bush Grenade Attacker Gets Life," CNN, January 11, 2006, http://www.cnn.com/2006/WORLD/europe/01/11/georgia.grenade/.

CNN, "Gulf War Fast Facts," CNN Library, July 30, 2019 https://www.cnn.com/2013/09/15/world/meast/gulf-war-fast-facts/index.html. Congressional Research Service, "The President's Management Agenda: A Brief Introduction," updated January 7, 2009, https://www.everycrsreport.com/reports/RS21416.html.

Cornell Law School Legal Information Institute 5 U.S. Code § 3331, Cornell Law School, Oath of office, accessed July 1, 2020, https://www.law.cornell.edu/uscode/text/5/3331.

Daggett, Stephen, "Costs of Major U.S. Wars," Congressional Research Service, June 29, 2010 https://fas.org/sgp/crs/natsec/RS22926.pdf.

The Economic Times, "China overtakes US in number of diplomatic missions," November 27, 2019, https://economictimes.indiatimes.com/news/international/world-news/china-overtakes-us-in-number-of-diplomatic-missions-study/articleshow/72258473.cms?utm_source=contentofinterest&utm_medium=text&utm_campaign=cppst.

Bibliography

Feigenbaum, Anna (2014, August 16), *100 Years of Tear Gas* A chemical weapon drifts off the battlefield and into the streets. Retrieved from https://www.theatlantic.com/international/archive/2014/08/100-years-of-tear-gas/378632/.

Gould, Joe, "Military brass defend State Department against White House budget ax," Defense News, October 30, 2018, https://www.defensenews.com/digital-show-dailies/sofic/2017/05/09/military-brass-defend-state-department-against-white-house-budget-ax/.

Guimond, Glen J., AFSA website "Examining State's Foreign Service Officer Hiring Today," American Foreign Service Association, accessed July 1, 2020 https://www.afsa.org/examining-states-foreign-service-officer-hiring-today.

Hadar, Roey and Gwen Ifill Fellow, "Key U.S. Ambassador Posts Remain Vacant," DISQUS. PBS, April 4, 2019, https://www.pbs.org/weta/washingtonweek/blog-post/key-us-ambassador-posts-remain-vacant.

Harris, Shane "Powell's Army," *Government Executive,* November 1, 2003, https://www.govexec.com/magazine/2003/11/powells-army/15328/.

Kerry, John, Remarks at the Chicago Council on Global Affairs, U.S. Department of State Archived Content, October 26, 2016, https://2009-2017.state.gov/secretary/remarks/2016/10/263653.htm.

Kopp, Harry, "Speaking Out," *The Foreign Service Journal,* American Foreign Service Association, January/February 2020, https://www.afsa.org/truth-and-honor.

Library of Congress, "Ukraine Famine," Revelations from the Russian Archives, accessed July 1, 2020, https://www.loc.gov/exhibits/archives/ukra.html

Manga, Dan, "Trump's Cabinet has been rocked by a number of ethics scandals — here's a complete guide," CNBC, updated February 16, 2018, https://www.cnbccom/2018/02/15/trump-cabinet-officials-in-ethics-scandals.html.

Markus, Vasyl and Ihor Stebelsky, "History of Ukraine, " The Internet Encyclopedia of Ukraine, accessed July 1, 2020, http://www.encyclopediaofukraine.com/display. asp?linkpath=pages%5CH%5CI%5CHistoryofUkraine.htm.

Marshall, Tabitha, "Oka Crisis," *The Canadian Encyclopedia,* July 11, 2016, https://www.thecanadianencyclopedia.ca/en/ article/oka-crisis.

Maskell, Jack, "Financial Disclosure by Federal Officials and Publication of Disclosure Reports," Congressional Research Service Report R43186, released August 22, 2013, https://fas.org/ sgp/crs/misc/R43186.pdf.

Nuclear Regulatory Commission, "U.S., Backgrounder on Chernobyl Nuclear Power Plant Accident," Nuclear Regulatory Commission Backgrounder, last updated August 15, 2018, https://www.nrc.gov/ reading-rm/doc-collections/fact-sheets/chernobyl-bg.html

Nelan, Bruce W., "Bear Hugs All Around," *Time,* January 24, 1994, pp. 38-41.

Palmer v. Shultz, 815 F.2d 84 (D.C. Cir. 1987), https://law.justia. com/cases/federal/appellate-courts/F2/815/84/22782/.

Savell, Stephanie, "America at War," *Smithsonian,* January 2019, https://www.smithsonianmag.com/history/ map-shows-places-world-where-us-military-operates-180970997/.

Selyukh, Alina and Lucia Maffei, "Who Oversees The President's Ethics? Here's Our List," National Pubic Radio, March 27, 2017, https://www.npr.org/2017/03/27/520983699/ who-oversees-the-president-s-ethics-a-reference-sheet.

Bibliography

Smith, R. Jeffrey, "Timeline: How Trump Withheld Ukraine Aid," the Center for Public Integrity #UKRAINEDOCS, December 13, 2019, https://publicintegrity.org/national-security/timeline-how-trump-withheld-ukraine-aid/.

Spiro, Peter J., "U.S. Supreme Court Knocks Down State Burma Law," American Society of International Law, June 3, 2000, https://www.asil.org/insights/volume/5/issue/7/us-supreme-court-knocks-down-state-burma-law.

Tiersky, Alex and Susan Epstein, "Securing U.S. Diplomatic Facilities and Personnel Abroad: Background and Policy Issues," Government Accounting Office Report 7-5700, July 30, 2014, https://fas.org/sgp/crs/row/R42834.pdf.

United Nations, Vienna Convention on Diplomatic Relations, Vienna, 18 April, 1961, United Nations Treaty Series, vol.330, No. 4739, p. 3, April 18, 1961, https://legal.un.org/ilc/texts/instruments/english/conventions/9_1_1961.pdf.

United Nations, "110 Governments Adopt Ambitious Global Programme to Tackle Marine Degradation," Meetings Coverage and Press Releases, Press Release HE/915, November 8, 1995, https://www.un.org/press/en/1995/19951108.he915.html.

U.S. Department of Defense, Defense Manpower Data Center (DMDC), DoD Personnel, Workforce Reports & Publications, accessed July 1, 2020, https://www.dmdc.osd.mil/appj/dwp/dwp_reports.jsp.

U.S. Department of Defense, National Defense Budget Estimates for FY 20201, April 2020, https://comptroller.defense.gov/Portals/45/Documents/defbudget/fy2021/FY21_Green_Book.pdf.

U.S. Government Spending, US Federal Budget Overview, accessed July 1, 2020, https://www.usgovernmentspending.com/federal_budget,

U.S. Department of Justice, Office of Public Affairs, "Malian National Sentenced to 25 Years in Prison for Conspiracy to Murder U.S. Diplomat," Press Release, April 26, 2016, April 26, https://www.justice.gov/opa/pr/malian-national-sentenced-25-years-prison-conspiracy-murder-us-diplomat.

U.S. Department of State, Bureau of Consular Affairs, "Diversity Visa Program - Entry," 2020, https://travel.state.gov/content/travel/en/us-visas/immigrate/diversity-visa-program-entry.html.

U.S. Department of State, Bureau of Consular Affairs, "Visa Waiver" Program, 2020, https://travel.state.gov/content/travel/en/us-visas/tourism-visit/visa-waiver-program.html.

U.S. Department of State, Bureau of Public Affairs, "Ukraine Relations," Fact Sheet, June 18, 1997, https://1997-2001.state.gov/regions/nis/fs-us_ukr_970618.html.

U.S. Department of State, The Foreign Affairs Manual for the US Department of State 2 FAM 070, Dissent Channel, CT:GEN-524, September 11, 2018,https://fam.state.gov/fam/02fam/02fam0070.html.

U.S. Department of State, "Facts About our Most Valuable Asset - Our People," Bureau of Human Resources Fact Sheet, March 31, 2019, https://www.state.gov/wp-content/uploads/2019/05/HR_Factsheet0319.pdf.

U.S. Department of State Office of the Historian, "The Rogers Act," accessed July 1, 2020, https://history.state.gov/departmenthistory/short-history/rogers.

U.S. Department of State, "U.S. Embassy Berlin, Backgrounder on the Pendleton Act," U.S. Embassy Berlin Backgrounder, accessed July 1, 2020, https://usa.usembassy.de/etexts/democrac/28.htm.

Bibliography

U.S. Office of Special Counsel (OSC), "Hatch Overview," OSC website definition, accessed July 1, 2020, https://osc.gov/Services/Pages/HatchAct.aspx.

Whitlock, Craig and Bob Woodward, "Pentagon buries evidence of $125 billion in bureaucratic waste. " *Washington Post*, December 5, 2016, https://www.washingtonpost.com/investigations/pentagon-buries-evidence-of-125-billion-in-bureaucratic-waste/2016/12/05/e0668c76-9af6-11e6-a0ed-ab0774c1eaa5_story.htm.

Woolf, Christopher, "Public Radio International, An ex-ambassador explains the 'dissent channel' that US diplomats are using to protest Trump's travel ban," The World, January 31, 2014, https://www.pri.org/stories/2017-01-31/ex-ambassador-explains-dissent-channel-us-diplomats-are-using-protest-trumps.

GLOSSARY OF TERMS

AFSA - American Foreign Service Association. The professional organization of the U.S. Foreign Service.

AAFSW - Associates of the American Foreign Service Worldwide. A non-governmental organization established in 1960 to support the Foreign Service community, with a focus on family members.

CAGs - Cleared American Guards. The security personnel responsible for the security of U.S. embassy construction sites.

Chargé - The person designated to assume the ambassador's duties when the ambassador is away from post.

CRS - Congressional Research Service. The organization that provides policy and legal analysis to both House and Senate committees and members, regardless of party affiliation.

CARE - Cooperative for Assistance and Relief Everywhere. A non-profit organization that focuses on poverty alleviation.

DAO - Defense Attaché Office or Officer. The chief U.S. military representation at a U.S. embassy.

DCM - Deputy Chief of Mission. The number two diplomatic position at a U.S. embassy or mission, after the ambassador.

DEA - Drug Enforcement Agency. A key U.S. law enforcement agency on drug trafficking and narcoterrorism issues.

Démarche - A petition that generally presents one government or international organization's point of view on an issue, along with a possible request for action on the issue to another government or international organization.

DRI - Diplomatic Readiness Initiative. The 2001 initiative by Secretary of State Colin Powell to fully fund and staff the U.S. Department of State. This initiative also focused on training and the use of new technology to make the Department more efficient and effective.

EFM - Eligible Family Member. The spouse of a member of the U.S. Foreign Service who is filling a job at a U.S. embassy, consulate, or mission.

FSN - Foreign Service National. FSNs are now called LES or Locally Engaged Staff, and are locally-hired personnel who work at U.S. embassies, consulates and other missions.

FSI - Foreign Service Institute. Now known as NFATC, or the National Foreign Affairs Training Center, this is the premier training institution for the U.S. Foreign Service.

GAO - Government Accountability Office. The office that collects, analyzes and reports on information about federal programs and services for the U.S. Congress.

IMF - International Monetary Fund - works to reduce poverty worldwide through cooperation on monetary policies and practices, focusing on international trade, sustainable economic growth and financial stability.

INL - Bureau of International Narcotics and Law Enforcement Affairs. The U.S. Department of State's lead bureau in the fight against drug trafficking and narcoterrorism.

KGB - Komitet Gosudarstvennoy Bezopasnosti (Committee for State Security). The secret police of the former Soviet Union

LES - Locally Engaged Staff. Formerly known as Foreign Service Nationals, these are locally-hired personnel who work at U.S. embassies, consulates and other missions.

MSG - Marine Security Guard. Marines who serve to protect U.S. embassies, and particularly, classified material.

NFATC - National Foreign Affairs Training Center, formerly known as FSI.

OES - Bureau of Oceans and International Environmental and Scientific Affairs. The U.S. Department of State's key bureau that provides leadership on environmental issues and works with economic partners to ensure sustainable economic development and protect the health of the planet.

OSC - The U.S. Office of Special Counsel. An independent federal investigative and prosecutorial agency that protects the United States' merit-based personnel system.

OMB - Office of Management and Budget. An office that reports directly to the president, and helps ensure that the president's policies and programs are carried out government-wide.

PMA - President's Management Agenda. President George W. Bush's 2001 initiative to make the U.S. federal government more efficient and effective.

RSC - Regional Support Center, Frankfurt Germany. The U.S. Department of States' office tasked with finding and providing military surplus items to the recently opened embassies in the former Soviet Union and other U.S. diplomatic missions that did not have the funding to procure needed furnishings, equipment and supplies.

Spetsnaz - Spetsialnovo Naznacheniya (special "purpose" or operations forces). A military group that was part of the former Soviet Union military intelligence forces.

TDY - Temporary duty assignment or officer. Personnel used to fill staffing gaps in regular two to three year positions, for example, when a regularly assigned officer is absent from post for an extended period for health or other reasons.

USAID - United States Agency for International Development. The U.S. federal government agency that provides and administers civilian foreign aid and development assistance to foreign countries.

USIA/USIS - United States Information Agency/Service. A formerly independent agency that is now part of the U.S. Department of States' Bureau of Public Affairs. It is responsible for public diplomacy overseas.

UNEP - UN Environmental Programme. The United Nations' program that provides leadership on environmental issues and works to ensure collaboration among nations to protect the health of the planet.

UNESCO - United Nations Educational, Scientific and Cultural Organization. A United Nations' specialized agency that works towards peace, poverty alleviation, sustainable development and cultural dialogue with a focus on education, the sciences, culture, communication and information. It is responsible for designating iconic landmarks as World Heritage Sites to help ensure their preservation.

INDEX

Index

Index

Index

Index

Index

Index